Tablespoons of Tears

Anna Marie

ISBN 978-0-9961146-2-2

Comments about Tablespoons of Tears and requests for additional copies, book club rates and author speaking appearances may be addressed to Blacktastic Books c/o Ms. McGhee, P.O. Box 235, Neptune, New Jersey, 07754, or you can send your comments and requests via website to www.blacktastic.net.

Dedication

This book is for women whose tears have run dry, leaving behind the imprint of existence, who have walked through the storm and learned to appreciate the smell of rain. For those who have fought battles without armor and who have claimed victory not for themselves but for others. Our character is formed by the fabric of our soul, not circumstance and what does not kill you will only make you stronger.

Table of Contents

My Yellow Brick Road

By

Anna Marie

Out of suffering have emerged the strongest souls; the most massive characters are seared with scars.

Khalil Gibran

Anna Marie

I.

The city was too big and my feet too small. Each square of concrete seemed to run the size of a football field, putting Los Angeles into a rare perspective. At this moment I could relate more to the world of ants as the street spanned for miles from my vantage point. Smog filled the air and the sunlight that seeped through its thickness was shadowed by the looming motels that traveled the length of the strip. Neon lights flashed the availability of vacancies or lack of them. All of these rooms, I know now, charged more often than not, by the hour.

****

I was five years old when we left the comforts of the four door sedan we had called home for the last two years, my brother and I. In the San Ysidro Park where we lived, all I remember was the playground. The faded teeter totters as they swung back and forth, shaped like dolphins and whales, wearing the painted outfits of what appeared to be bellboys, complete with matching hats. Even then, I questioned the meaning of their attire. The wooden play structure in the midst of a sea of sand was the highlight of my day and would occupy my mind for hours. It often drew my attention away from the booming voice of my father as he seemed to find yet another of my mother's shortcomings. Their arguments were mostly one sided, my father flying off the handle about one thing or another and my mother, with her head bowed would wait for the storm to pass. I wish from her I would have learned more patience and less submission.

There has always been the straw the broke the camel's back, the nail in the coffin so to speak. Though at such a young age I hadn't

3

yet familiarized myself with those specific phrases. They say it never rains in Southern California but I had indeed weathered my share of metaphorical storms. As I recall it was mid-day, the sun perhaps at its highest peak in the sky, the birds chirping, setting the scene for a perfect afternoon aside from the sudden screams of our mother. Her high pitched wail from inside the vehicle snapped our heads abruptly toward the commotion and our feet started moving in the direction of the car before we could give it a second thought.

She remained huddled in the corner, face pressed against the glass as a small child drawn to a window display yet instead of delight, her face was painted with grief and agony. My eyes first traveled to her hand grasping her thigh where the crimson stain had begun seeping through her brown pant leg and then wandered to the broken glass shards scattered on the faded leather seat and floorboards. Milk had sprayed all over the interior, dripping like clouded raindrops down the dashboard and upholstery.

He had said that the glass she gave him was unwashed, smelled of filth and was still shouting obscenities. This wasn't the first time I had witnessed this accusation or reaction from my father. He was a man of pride, a conspiracy theorist, demanded respect and could have by others, been labeled a tyrant. My brother and I endured more spankings as he called them, down playing their severity, before school age than most were accustomed to their entire lives. He spared no rod and spoiled no child, definitely not his own.

We were quickly instructed to "stay out of grown folks business" and shooed away with tears in our eyes and concern for our mother written all over our faces. We whispered to each other between sobs, barely catching our breath as we spoke of injustice and abuse, though I'm sure those weren't our exact words. A plan was derived in a matter of minutes. We both agreed we had grown tired of the arguments that had been woven into our lives like a part of our anatomy. Even without having regular access to televisions we had seen enough of normal family life to know we were not a part of one.

It was my idea. At the time I could not foresee the future, had not thought it through and had no idea that the grass would not be greener on the other side. I envisioned perhaps a soft carpet the color of emeralds, plush and its touch cool to the skin under my bare feet. The highway was just beyond the entrance to the park and we waited. We waited until their raised voices shifted into subtle snores as they took their mid afternoon nap curled in the front seat of the blue Buick. My brother and I took no belongings with us, only hope. We packed all the bad memories away and set off in search of something more, perhaps the opportunity to be children.

At first, it seemed like another one of our many adventures we had already experienced in our unconventional childhood. The anticipation of the unknown was thrilling but reality started to seep in through the cracks. No one in their right mind would even think of stopping to pick up two lanky kids, malnourished and dressed in tattered, faded and mismatched clothes. We had runaways written all over our faces. The park was huge but we had still taken no chance of being seen by anyone who knew our parents whereabouts to alert them. So we chose to walk over a mile down the highway before starting our poor attempt at hitch hiking. We stood there, on the side of the road, thumbs sticking out as the cars passed us by in droves.

As the sun descended behind the trees and the temperature began to drop, we began to question our decision and our sanity. I started to cry, asking if maybe we should just go home but my brother was right, it was too late now. They would most likely both be awake and had probably already started looking for us. At this point, my greatest fear had become the beating we would have waiting for us if had decided to return.

Over an hour had passed before the big rig pulled to the shoulder, brakes squealing and flashing its hazards as it slowed to a stop in front of us. Its mass loomed over us like a mechanical tower, our faces illuminated by the slow blinking of the amber lights displaying our fear in short bursts. We hesitated, both weary of the situation, knowing there would be no retreat once we entered and were carried away from our so called home. We held each other's hands and approached the passenger door with caution. Looking back over our shoulders almost hoping our parents would be running towards us with smiles on their faces and apologies on their tongues.

The driver was in his early forties with missing teeth and warm eyes. He looked down from the cab of the eighteen-wheeler with an inquisitive frown.

"What're you kids doin' out on this road alone?" he asked, voice thick with chewing tobacco and a southern accent.

With the time we spent waiting for our, would be getaway vehicle, we had derived a story in our underdeveloped minds that would be acceptable to very few. Luckily, this man whom apparently had more compassion than common sense ended up buying it like it was the last item on sale.

My brother spoke steadily although I could feel his pulse racing through the palm of his hand as I tightened my grip. He told him our concocted story about a sick aunt who had been hospitalized and us trying desperately to get home to our parents in Los Angeles. The man ate it up like he was starving and my brother's words were Sunday dinner.

"Well, climb on up, ya here. I'll take you as far as I can but I ain't goin' all the way in to the big city." He smiled, moving his bag of empty Styrofoam boxes from the passenger seat and discarded them behind his into the cab portion of the truck to make room for the two of us.

At twelve years old, my brother stood tall and had more courage and better conversation than men twice his age. I remember being proud and feeling protected as he positioned himself between me and the driver, reaching over to fasten my seatbelt.

"It'll be alright, little sis, I won't let anything bad happen to you." He whispered, his breath tickling my ear and making the hairs on the back of my neck rise.

The man said his name was Walter, that he had two kids "right 'bout y'all age", and would be glad to help us out. Saying over and over again how worried sick our parents must be. After about forty-five minutes on the road, we stopped at a diner and he bought us dinner consisting of a burger, fries and a milkshake. I opted for strawberry while my brother chose vanilla. We ate the food greedily, stuffing our mouths as if it would be taken from us as quickly as it had been given or as if he would have changed his mind about the offer in the midst of a bite. He stopped eating his double cheeseburger just to watch us scarf down our meals almost in awe.

"You younguns' sure were hungry, weren't ya?"

We nodded, unable to speak for fear of risking even a morsel of food out of our mouths by replying. When you go days without eating, you learn to appreciate even the crumbs. We couldn't tell him we hadn't eaten since Monday morning when here it was Tuesday night. The milk my father had wasted was the last we had left over from the half gallon purchased over the weekend. Then, we had indulged on Goobers brand peanut butter and jelly sandwiches, the kind that came with both products in the same jar, easily consolidated and cost effective. We couldn't tell him we had never had a cheeseburger.

I was getting full as my stomach was quite disproportioned due to lack of consistent meals and I looked longingly at the remainder of fries on my plate. Waiting until Walter turned his eyes away from us I stuffed them into my jacket pocket earning a frown of disgust from the customer two tables over. She shook her head in disapproval and rolled her eyes.

She obviously could tell we were no kin to Walter with his sandy brown hair spotted with grey and blue eyes. My brother Darnell and I bore a darker skin tone and we both wore our thick ringlets in an afro surrounding our thin faces. My mother, of German and Swedish decent, had never mastered the art of black hair care and even if she had, we had no money to purchase the products needed to make ours manageable. I was somewhat of an odd looking child with large front teeth that housed a gap big enough to fit a steam engine through and a widow's peak that descended into my large forehead.

Darnell was attractive for a youth and looked much older than his age. He had grown into his frame well and didn't appear as awkward in his oversized corduroys and pea coat as I did in my second hand, hand me downs. That was the down side of being the younger sibling, especially to the opposite sex. I had been mistaken for a boy on more than one occasion, stuck wearing his faded blue jeans and button up shirts. I was a tomboy by choice but also had a deep seated longing for frilly dresses and colored ribbons.

After our meal we got back in the cab portion of the eighteen-wheeler and Walter let us explore his sleeping quarters which he had made quite comfortable considering it was as small as a bathroom only lacking the amenities. He explained that he drove cross country for a living and often would give those less fortunate, rides to their destination. Apparently we were his youngest passengers thus far but clearly the best company. He flashed us a grin that showed off his remaining teeth, stained yellow most likely from too much coffee and cigarettes.

Walter gathered some additional blankets from a box he kept in his storage area and surrendered the small cramped bed to us for the remainder of the night. He snored lightly from the driver's seat; his body crouched behind the steering wheel in obvious discomfort. We laid there motionless and tense until morning, neither of us sleeping.

We were sad for the time we spent with him to come to an end but as we neared his drop off location he stated that he couldn't arrive with any additional baggage, referring to us. He stopped at a local store to purchase snacks for the remainder of our trip and bid us farewell at the next truck stop. We sat huddled in the small booth drinking cups of hot chocolate my brother had purchased with the pocket change Walter had given him, wondering what would be next on our adlibbed agenda.

We had chosen Los Angeles, maybe because it was the city of dreams or maybe just because it was a city we had both heard of and not an unreasonable distance from our starting point. We knew no one that lived there and had no idea what we would do when we arrived. As the day became brighter and warmth began to reach in through the grimy window of the café, we decided it was time to continue our journey. Stepping again into the elements, the air smelled of diesel and cigarette smoke. We found ourselves traveling down the highway once more with our thumbs propositioning cars that welcomed us with only the winds of their velocity and disappointment.

We ended up walking much further than we had initially and my legs were growing achy and tired. I had begun complaining, whining and wanting to go home, which my brother was having no part of. Neither of us had a watch so we didn't know how much time had passed but judging from the positioning of the sun, it was approaching twilight.

The green pinto pulled over in front of us swerving and stopped abruptly, stirring up a cloud of dust that blurred our vision and sent us both into a coughing fit. Instead of waiting for us to approach, the driver hopped out and headed our way. He was tall, skinny with dark skin and a flashy smile. He wore a jean jacket with his eyes hidden by shades and his afro by a red beret cocked to one side. He sauntered toward us, long arms swinging beside him in a rhythmic gait.

"Y'all kids need a ride?" he asked.

"Yeah" my brother spoke hesitantly "We're headed into the city." mimicking the phrase he had picked up from Walter "our parents are waiting for us there."

"We'll c'mon, y'all can roll with me.   Lucky I saw ya, I almost passed you up." He replied.

I climbed in the back while my brother rode shotgun. The car smelled damp, musty and in order for me to take a seat, I found myself clearing beer cans and other trash out of the way.

"Don't mind the mess, Baby Girl, this my bro's car. I'm just borrowin' it and he don't care what it look like." He laughed "Wasn't plannin' on havin' company though.   As a matter of fact, I gotta make a couple stops before I drop y'all where you need to be."

He turned up the radio. Donna Summer's Last Chance blared from the speakers. He bobbed his head along to the music as I surveyed my immediate surroundings. There were jackets and clothes strewn across the seat, crumpled newspapers and what appeared to be piles of mail crowding the area on the floor where I had placed my feet, along with the multitude of cans and fast food bags.

"The name's Leroy." He said, not turning his eyes from the road. "So why don't y'all tell me your names and what you really doin' out here."

Our response was silence. Darnell and I looked at each other nervously and thought about relaying the same scenario but we both knew we wouldn't have gotten the same reaction. I caught a glimpse of Leroy in the rearview mirror, his eyes were still hidden from sight by his dark gasses but I knew he had seen me looking. I immediately put my head down and started fidgeting with my fingers.   I remembered the now cold french fries I had stashed in my jacket pocket and dug them out. Making sure there was no lint, I began to eat them silently. I had counted eight in all.

My brother looked out the window at the passing lights and highway signs. I knew in his mind he was trying to decide whether to tell the truth or to stick with the plan. Leroy didn't seem like the type to go running to the cops. Actually, he seemed more the kind to be headed in the opposite direction. Ends up, Darnell didn't have to say much either way.

"Let's just cut to the chase," Leroy said, lowering his sunglasses down the length of his nose, this time meeting my eyes in the mirror. "I know y'all runaways, I seen ya' kind a million times before. So what's the plan? You got anywhere to go?"

My brother shifted uneasily in his seat. I started to cry, which always seemed to be my default reaction, like a bad catch phrase. Leroy reached over and opened the glove box, retrieving an opened pack of Newports from within and lit up. My brother and I both scrunched our nose up at the smell, one thing we were not accustomed to as neither of my parents had taken up the habit of smoking cigarettes. He took a long drag, the cherry growing brighter as he inhaled the thick smoke.

"I'll let y'all take ya time to tell me, just tryin' to help."

Nobody spoke for the next few miles. We decided in unison to let Anita Baker do the talking. It had started to rain. The water drops gathering on the window were refracting the colors of the streetlights as we approached the city. I had seen nothing like it before, through all our travels we had never been to Los Angeles or any city of its grandeur. The buildings were massive and breathtaking. I had always pictured myself being here, but walking the red carpet instead of riding in the back of a beat up pinto, a little girl with big dreams.

My brother finally broke the silence.

"My name's Johnny and my little sister is Bessie" he lied, my name was Anna last time I checked, and where on earth would he have gotten that name from "and no, we don't have anywhere to go." He held his head down, studying his shoelaces intently.

"Ha ha! That's what I thought. You can't fool Leroy. Well, nice to meet ya. I tell ya what, you can stay the night with me. I gotta run a few errands first but I'm a help y'all out. Us brothas gotta stick together, right my man?" He slapped my brother on his back and laughed loudly.

Something in his tone just didn't seem right but I couldn't quite put my finger on it. We passed a majority of the city before taking an off ramp into a more secluded part of town. Here the buildings were less impressive with mostly single story residences and dilapidated fences displaying colorful graffiti art. After a number of lefts and rights, Leroy pulled the car up to a house surrounded by a chain link fence with several big wheels and other toys displayed on the front yard. A beware of dog sign hung just inside the front gate.

"I'll be right back. Y'all sit tight and stay in the car." He turned the keys taking them out of the ignition, looked around then opened the door and locked it behind him.

The street seemed to have suddenly become busy with crowds of people walking past us on both sides of the car oblivious to the rain. Most paid us no mind though some stopped to peek in the window laughing before continuing on their way. Leroy's right back ended up being close to an hour. He returned, smelling of liquor and in a much less pleasant mood then when he left us. He fumbled the keys trying to unlock the door and dropped them under the car, muttering curse words under his breath. My brother reached over and pulled up the latch for him, earning him only a scowl.

"I'm droppin' y'all off at my place, you gonna have to stay there 'til I get back."

He revved the engine, doing what I assumed were donuts getting us turned around in the right direction and back on the freeway. After quite a few exits we found ourselves in the midst of the city which had appeared to be much more glamorous from afar. Up close and personal, trash littered the streets and the homeless huddled in doorways with their shopping carts and boxes trying to stay out of the rain. He pulled into an alleyway and then into a parking garage. The vertical climb in the pinto seemed almost tedious or maybe I just hadn't noticed the poor condition of the car as most of the trip was spent with the music blaring.

He found a parking spot in between an old moving van and a grey Cadillac, parking so close to the sedan we all had to climb out the driver's side door. He locked the car and we followed him to the shabby elevator through the dimly lit garage. The small unit smelled strongly of urine and as we descended into the main lobby of what ended up being a hotel, I held my breath. Leroy opened a door and we trailed at his heels like puppy dogs. Darnell and I exchanged glances unsure of what we had gotten ourselves into and my fear was mounting at an increasing rate.

We turned the corner into a small lobby that housed only a small desk and vending machines stacked against an adjacent wall. The wallpaper was the color of vomit and peeling. My pulse quickened as an older Hispanic man with a handlebar moustache turned his attention away from the black and white thirteen inch screen on the desk to scowl at us. Placing his cigarette in the astray he started in on Leroy.

"Leroy, what the fuck!" he yelled "First you three weeks late wit da rent then you bring kids up in here? Kids, Leroy?"

"Javier, my man, just chill" Leroy replied "this my niece and nephew, they only gon' be here for a few days. You scarin' em. I told you, I got your money Friday. I been outta town, just got in tonight."

"You better have my shit, man, or I'll throw your ass out. I got no problem wit that! Oh yeah, Candy's upstairs, she been lookin' for you."

Leroy hunched down and whispered in our ears, wrapping his arms around our shoulders.

"Don't you worry 'bout him, he's harmless, wouldn't hurt a fly."

We glanced back at Javier behind the desk who had turned his attention back to his program with our minds full of doubt but neither of us would dare call Leroy a liar. We took the stairs up one flight and ventured down another lime green corridor, its walls faded and stained from water damage. There were a multitude of doors on both sides, their brass numbers crooked and in dire need of polishing. The brown shag carpet was torn, dirty and matted in many places. He stopped in front of room 219 and dug deep into his pockets for the key.

When the door opened, we found the room in a worse condition than the rest of the establishment and we were greeted by a thick cloud of smoke. A blonde woman, supposedly Candy, lay across the unmade bed reading a Glamour magazine which she should have used as a study guide and been taking notes. Her stonewashed jeans were ripped, about two sizes too small and were accompanied but what appeared to be no more than a turquoise bra. She smiled at us with thick burgundy lips and batted her eyes adorned with so much blue eye shadow it appeared to make the simple act of blinking a hard thing to do.

"Whatcha got here, Leroy?" She asked, her voice thick and sultry.

"This my niece and nephew. What you doin' here girl?"

"Tony said you'd have somethin' for me."

"I just got back. Tell Tony I'll get with him later. Right now, I need some, uh, family time" he motioned toward the still open door.

She frowned obviously not liking the response she was getting, grabbed her faux fur coat from the TV stand and walked past us, leaving my brother and I choking on cheap perfume. The room was small and dirty with holes in the carpeting and thin drapes covering the only window. Neither one of us dared move a muscle or take another breath until we were sure the air was clear. Leroy closed the door behind her and went into what appeared to be the bathroom giving us an opportunity to survey our temporary home.

I put my arms around Darnell and buried my face in his shirt. This was nothing like what I had in mind and the only thing I wanted now were the comforts of familiar insecurity. I regretted leaving and wanted to go home. He held me and stroked my curly hair, his fingers getting caught in its tangles. Leroy came out of the small room and sat down on the bed looking us up and down.

"Y'all want somethin' to eat?" he asked.

We nodded in unison. We hadn't eaten anything since the snacks Walter had bought us and my eight fries had already run their course. He motioned us to sit down on the bed, stating he would be right back and we again, found ourselves alone. The bed was hard and lumpy, the sheets were thin and worn and the entire room smelled like body odor and feet. Darnell attempted to turn on the television but couldn't get anything to appear on the screen so he gave up. He handed me the Glamour magazine Candy had left behind in haste and I flipped through it. We didn't have much to say to each other, both feeling somewhat in limbo.

At five years old, my mother had already started home schooling and I could read fairly well so I gave my best attempt at an article about fashion do's and don'ts. Leroy didn't take long at all, returning with bags of chips and candy bars he had managed to cop from the downstairs vending machine. We didn't complain. Junk food was something we had never been allowed to eat so we were more than happy for our dinner to consist of chocolate and Cheetos. We washed it down with cans of Coca Cola and for a moment forgot about our troubles.

After we had stuffed ourselves to the point of no return, Leroy announced he had one more errand to tend to and needed Johnny to accompany him. "Man business" he stated.

Darnell refused outright, saying he couldn't leave me.

"She's only five, Leroy, she can't stay here by herself!" he protested.

"She'll be fine, I'll have Javier come up and check on her. I need you to help me out with somethin'. C'mon man. Anyways, you old enough to know, ain't nothin' in life free and I'm givin' y'all a place to stay. How old are ya anyways?"

"I'm fifteen" he lied.

"Well kid, you gon' need some money to take care of Baby Girl and I got a job for ya. She'll be fine and we won't be gone but a half an hour, she probably need a nap anyway."

Leroy had won by default and it happened so fast I couldn't catch up. Darnell kissed me on the forehead and swore he would be right back, saying Leroy was right, if he was going take care of us he needed money and Leroy was offering to help. The door closed and I found myself alone, really alone for the first time ever. No matter what, Darnell had always been there. Even when my parents would abandon us for days, they left me in his capable hands and he had never let anything happen to me.

The room that appeared small at first seemed to double in size and I attempted to lie down, close my eyes and imagine myself anywhere else but here. It was cold so I climbed under the sheets and dingy blanket curling my small frame into a ball. I must have nodded off for an hour or so and awoke with a start. I had completely forgotten where I was, my surroundings were foreign and when my memory was jogged the fear became even worse. Darnell still hadn't returned. The tears fell like a dam breaking, my sobs were loud, uncontrollable and I had to pee yet couldn't bring myself to leave the bed.

After a good five minutes of psyching myself up, I mustered the courage to tip toe to the room where Leroy had vanished off to when we first arrived, only to find a sink and hand towels. No toilet. I stared in disbelief. It wasn't only the lack of a toilet that sent me over the edge. Climbing the walls were several large cockroaches that appeared to be coming out of a hole positioned behind the sink. I stifled a scream and slammed the door shut.

There was another door in the small room but who in their right mind would build a sink in one room and a toilet in the other and after what was discovered in the first, I was afraid to open it. My need to urinate stronger than my fear, I ran to the second door, my little feet padding on the hard floor. For all the shag carpeting in the hallway there was nothing more than a thin layer in the rooms, if that. I opened the door carefully, a closet, just as I had originally thought. Where was the toilet?

I sat down on the bed and began rocking back and forth, tears streaming down my face and my nose running. Since there was no toilet that meant no toilet paper so I wiped it with the back of my sleeve. Where was Darnell and more importantly at that specific time, where was the bathroom? I was scared but the urge hadn't subsided and was not showing any signs of doing so. I crept to the door leading to the hallway. I was afraid of running into Javier, who Leroy said wouldn't hurt a fly but seemed likely to eat little children for breakfast.

I peered outside and was greeted with flickering lights that ricocheted off the vomit green walls giving the corridor an eerie appearance. I looked back in the direction from which we came and saw the door leading to the stairs where Javier surely awaited with a knife, fork and a big appetite. In the other direction I saw another door at the end of the hall slightly ajar and could make out a glimpse of linoleum. I stepped outside, careful to not shut the door to the room all the way for fear of being locked out although I had to weigh

becoming saturated with saliva and was making me even colder. I still had to pee.

"Mommy" I cried out, drawing the attention of the pedestrians within earshot, who glanced my way but did nothing more. "Mommy?"

I knew she wasn't there, couldn't hear me and that my outburst was in vain. I turned on my heels, looking up at the large marquee above me but from my view I couldn't see the name of the hotel. I would have had to step away, into the street to be able to read the sign. I gave up, walking at a slow pace back into the seedy lobby. Javier was waiting behind the desk.

"What you doin' down here, missy? Ain't Leroy tell you stay put?"

"There's no toilet paper!" I blurted out, running back up the stairs to my not so safe haven.

I didn't stop until I reached the door to the room which this time I found locked. I jangled the handle and kicked the door. This couldn't be happening. I had been so careful not to shut it last night but had completely forgotten this morning. I glanced over my shoulder expecting to see the massive frame of Javier in the entryway to the stairs searching for his next meal but there was no one. I sat down on the musty carpet, my back to the door and my head between my knees sobbing. My eyes were sore from too much crying and I had a huge lump in my throat.

It must have been only a few minutes before I felt a presence standing over me. Javier had approached quietly because I didn't hear the door to the stairwell open or his footsteps. He handed me a roll of toilet paper.

"Where's that boy that was with you?" he asked.

"He went with Leroy last night and never came back." My voice was breaking, barely audible.

"Don't worry, girl. Leroy won't let nothin' happen to him. Go on, go potty" He told me, pointing in the direction of the bathroom.

I took the roll of tissue paper and headed down the hall. I could hear keys jingling as he retrieved what must have been a master set from his pocket. When I reached the bathroom, I cracked the door open proceeding with caution. Thankfully the presence of the roaches wasn't as prominent as before and now, with toilet paper, the whole process went a lot smoother.

When I returned to the room I found Javier stooped over wrestling with the knobs on the TV. He had managed to get a picture, lined and with bad reception but whatever was airing was much better then staring at the discolored and peeling wallpaper. I sat on the edge of the bed as he continued to fiddle with the monitor.

"You hungry, mejita?" he asked, not looking up from his task.

"Yes, a little" I replied shyly, still sniffling. Actually I was starving.

He turned away from the screen and looked at me puzzled. Shaking his head he stood, turned toward the door and left. I remained on the bed, still free and clear of any blankets, sheets or bugs and wrapped my arms around my torso, hugging myself tightly. What if he was somewhere hurt, I thought. Leroy seemed nice enough but then first impressions weren't always accurate. Look at Javier, I had thought the worst of him and he ended up being not so bad after all. My mind wandered through many different scenarios of what could have happened to Darnell. When I had just about exhausted all options and scared myself half to death, Javier returned through the doorway with a Styrofoam container and a small plastic bag.

"You like pancakes?" he asked, setting the food down next to me on the bed.

I nodded. What kid in their right mind didn't like pancakes? It's funny, I never associated food with the taste, only the way it looked and smelled. We had spent several nights in diners sleeping in the booths, watching the other patrons eat and inhaling their plates as the waitresses passed us by. My brother and I would hold conversations not about what we would own when we were rich and famous but what foods we would order. Eventually the manager would approach my father with the ultimatum to either purchase something or to leave. I learned that sometimes a single cup of coffee would go a long way.

The plastic bag contained butter, syrup, a plastic knife and fork wrapped in cellophane, and a half pint carton of milk. Opening the Styrofoam container the aroma was like heaven, the three large buttermilk pancakes were warm and as perfect as the ones on the Aunt Jemima box. I looked up at Javier with tears in my eyes.

"Thank you" I squeaked out.

As hungry as I was, I couldn't finish even a single pancake. All I was thinking about was if Darnell had eaten this morning and my guilt made each bite hard to swallow. I shut the lid to the box deciding to save some for him when he arrived. My carton of milk still half full I closed the top flaps, folding them over to keep the contents fresh and made a neat stack of all the items on the top of the television set. I was afraid of any of the cockroaches getting a whiff and going into attack mode.

Javier had left me to eat in peace, managing to get the TV to work fairly well before making his exit. The Flintstones were on and I found myself laughing, then immediately covering my mouth, feeling ashamed for finding humor in anything when I still had no idea of my brother's whereabouts. I watched the rest of the episode in silence, not even risking a smile, my mind again elsewhere.

I must have dozed off once more for I was awakened by the creaking of the motel room door and Leroy's laughter. I jumped off the bed and ran into Darnell's waiting arms as he scooped me up and twirled me around in circles. I buried my face in the crook of his neck suppressing the urge to again burst into tears.

"See, now I told ya' they be trippin' but they always come back...always. You'll see, stick with me, my man and you'll learn somethin'" Leroy kicked off his shoes and sat down, retrieving a fresh pack of cigarettes from his shirt pocket. "and look at Baby Girl, she doin' just fine."

I scowled at him, lacking the ferocity intended in my gaze as I was too filled with relief having my brother back safe and sound. Leroy lit the cigarette, balanced it between his lips and squinted his eyes to avoid the rising smoke. He reached in the pocket of his pants and pulled out a wad of papers and other items entwined with various bills and strolled over to the little room containing the sink.

"Y'all keep yourself outta trouble."

My bother took a seat at the end of the bed, kicking the rumpled covers aside and motioned for me to join him. He pulled a stack of bills out of his own pocket. It was more money than I had ever seen but in actuality, only thirty-two dollars.

"Look sis, Leroy said I get to keep it and there's more where this came from."

"What did you do?" my eyes growing bigger. I didn't have a good feeling about this.

"Nothing really bad or anything like that but we're gonna be alright. I told you I won't let anything happen to you." He replied, laying back on the mattress and counting his wages.

I walked to the TV stand; retrieving the breakfast I had saved him from on top of the small set and began to tell him about my adventures while he had been away. He listened intently between bites. He laughed at my fear of cockroaches, reassuring me that they didn't bite and frowned when I told him about my experience on the street. He was obviously upset I had ventured out on my own.

Leroy stepped from the washroom, the best name I had for it, closing the door behind him and sweating profusely. Walking to the window he pulled aside the worn curtain just slightly, peering down into the alley below. He lit another cigarette and mumbled to himself under his breath. Darnell and I watched him quietly. He had no idea that he had become the sole focal point of our attention but something in his demeanor had changed and we both had taken note of it.

"Y'all can't stay here. I gotta friend that'll probably take ya in but this here ain't gonna work. Ay, yo Johnny, I'm a need you to put in some more work if ya want Baby Girl to have a place to stay. Time to grow up, son. Life ain't never been easy." He scratched his head, not making eye contact. "I gotta make a few calls, y'all sit tight." he said, stopping to put on his shoes then walked out the door in a plume of smoke.

"What does he mean, Darnell? Where are we gonna go?" I asked fearfully.

"I don't know, Anna" he replied, sounding worried.

"Darnell, I don't like this, I wanna go home. I want Mommy." I started whining.

He shot me a look out of the corner of his eye. I sniffed, trying not to cry. I knew we were way too far from home and that he was trying his best to keep his composure but deep down inside he must have been as scared as I was. Thirty-two dollars wouldn't fix that.

"You do remember this was your idea right?" he reminded me.

That wasn't the consolation I was looking for. I sat on the bed swinging my legs back and forth, placing my right hand in my mouth and started biting my nails. One of my many nervous habits I had developed trying to cope with a harsh reality I should have never had to face at such a young age. He paced back and forth while I just watched, counting his footsteps.

Leroy returned, headed back to the washroom without a word and after a few minutes, emerged, grabbed his jacket from where he had discarded it on the floor and headed back toward the door.

"Let's go."

We followed him in silence, almost breaking into a run just to keep up. The pancakes remained on the bed, half eaten and the milk carton untouched. It seemed like the longest journey down the stairs and back into the hotel lobby which I couldn't say I would miss. Javier took his attention away from the airing of The Price is Right long enough to give me a quick wink as we headed down the long corridor leading to the parking garage.

Luckily this time he had found a parking spot on the first floor so we managed to avoid the putrid smelling elevator altogether. As we climbed into the pinto, I for only the second time, Darnell asked him where we were going.

"I'm gonna take your sis to my girl Shirley's crib but she ain't got room for no teenage boys, so you gonna have to hang with me." He said, looking in the rearview as he pulled out of the space, careful not to scrape the paint off a black pickup truck he had once again, parked dangerously close to.

I started to protest and Darnell gave me a look that said in so many words to keep my mouth shut. I swallowed the lump in my throat and let him do the talking.

"Look Leroy, I can't just leave her alone with strange people, she's too little for that."

"Unless ya want her out on the street, that's where she gon' be. Shirley the only one'll take her in. Maybe y'all shoulda though about that before ya ran away, don't ya think? Don't worry, she ain't gon' be that far, you can go see her anytime you want." He laughed; putting his shades back on and turning up the volume on the radio, signifying that he was done with the conversation.

We drove for about ten minutes before pulling up to a pale pink house with a tetherball pole in the front yard and landscaping that was in desperate need of a manicure. The grass that remained was patchy and littered with trash. There were two cars in the driveway, more accurately one and a half. The chassis of a gray pickup up truck sat on blocks with the bed portion completely removed. The homes in the surrounding area were in no better shape and all of the houses were in dire need of paint.

"Stay here" he told us, turning off the ignition and exiting the car.

We watched him approach the front door which was halfway ajar and saw the frame of a tall woman with big hair join him in the entryway. She appeared to be about fortyish with a large build and was dressed in a gaudy purple muumuu reminiscent of the outfits Mrs. Roper used to wear on the TV series Three's Company. I could see bright colors flashing across her face all the way from where I sat in the car which reminded me of Leroy's friend, Candy. I wondered if they studied from the same issue of Glamour.

Leroy kept looking over his shoulder and I could see the woman straining her neck trying to get a glimpse of us. We both sat back in our seats attempting to stay out of view. I wasn't sure why, apparently this would be my final destination. I started to cry, wiping my nose on the back of my sleeve. In my mind I could hear my mother's disapproval though given our situation I'm sure she would have been worried about bigger problems than my personal hygiene.

Gesturing their arms they beckoned us to join them. Reluctantly we slid out of the vehicle and trudged up the concrete walkway. I kept my head down, trying to hide the tears that rolled down my face like rain, dragging my feet on the pavement as I went. The storm had passed through the night giving way to an overcast and gray sky which did nothing to lighten my spirits. My brother reached for my hand. As I wrapped my fingers around his, I could feel their warmth and somehow felt that this would be the last time I would see him for quite a while.

"Pick ya head up, child" she said, cupping my face in her hands when I finally made it within her reach. Her pale fingers were short and stubby with bright red nails almost two inches in length, their color clashing badly with her skin tone and her attire. I winced, her hands were cold and clammy yet I obeyed, looking up into her watery green eyes which showed no sign of compassion.

"Leroy tell me you only seven and your Mama done left you. Now why a woman do that to a sweet kid like you?" She glanced at Darnell "You must be Johnny he been telling me so much about. Don't you worry none, I'm a take good care of your sis, here."

Darnell looked down, stuffing his hands in his pockets. Shirley guided the both of us inside and Leroy followed. The interior of the house was even worse than outside. The living room was decorated with two shabby couches, tan in color or perhaps appearing so from lack of steam cleaning and a coffee table which even though had all four, appeared to be on its last leg. There were toys and dirty laundry gathered in piles on the floor. Three small bookshelves that cased dusty china dolls and a variety of other knick knacks lined the otherwise vacant walls. A wooden floor model television was positioned kitty corner in the small area.

I could get a view of the kitchen from where I stood trembling. Dishes were piled up in the sink and the trash can next to what I assumed was a good size pantry, spilled over and onto the linoleum. A tiny square table stood in the middle of the dining area and was cluttered with boxes of cereal, bowls and newspapers.

"My kids still in school," she said "I got two girls a little older than you, Rosa and Bianca. They'll be home in a few hours and you can meet them then."

I didn't want to meet them. I just wanted my brother not to leave which I knew would be happening in a matter of minutes. Leroy was starting to get impatient and kept looking at his watch. She took me down a hallway with picture frames housing what must have been old family photos hanging crooked on the walls. Their stained yellow color reminded me of Walter's teeth and gave the wallpaper at the hotel a run for its money. She cracked open the door to a room much cleaner than the rest of the house displaying a set of bunk beds adorned with stuffed animals and cabbage patch dolls.

"You can sleep with my girls" she stated, shutting it as she ventured down the rest of the hallway.

"Hey, we gotta get goin' Shirley" Leroy tapped his foot impatiently "she cool here, right?"

"Yeah, you gonna bring me the money tomorrow? She asked.

He shook his head, yes, motioning my brother and I to say our goodbyes. I swallowed hard, tears streaming down my face as I threw my arms around his waist and held on to him for dear life. He bent down whispering in my ear.

"Leroy said I can come back in the morning. Shhh sis, don't cry, she seems real nice, I promise I'll see you tomorrow." He gave me a kiss on the forehead, pried my arms from his thin body and trailed Leroy out the front door. My eyes followed them as they headed down the concrete walkway. I remained leaning against the wood frame of the open door, whimpering, watching the pinto minimize in size until it disappeared completely.

II.

"C'mon Bessie, hush that noise," Shirley said "go on get you some cereal, look on the table in the kitchen. We gonna get you in school real soon, can't be sittin' here with me all day. Gotta get your education" she laughed, sitting on one of the couches, turning her attention away from me and back to her soap opera.

I had forgotten my name had been changed to protect the innocent and I just recently learned I had aged two years in a day. So far being seven wasn't all it was cracked up to be. I walked over to the small table and surveyed my options. Captain Crunch, Trix and Froot Loops. I was momentarily in junk food heaven. I hadn't even been hungry until now and the sweet smell of sugar filled my nostrils from the half open boxes.

I looked around the kitchen wondering where the bowls and utensils were kept. I couldn't wait to sample them all but knew, since I was probably going to be here for a while, I could take my time. I peered around the corner to see Shirley staring intently at the TV set, biting her nails.

"Miss Shirley," I asked, barely audible "Where are the bowls and spoons?"

"You see that sink a dishes, girl. Wash somethin' out" she replied, scoffing "I hope you ain't think I'm gonna be your maid. Listen here, Leroy payin' me good money to keep an eye on you. Not doin' this out the goodness of my heart, sunshine."

Her laughter was harsh and thick like molasses. It had only been about ten minutes at the most since Leroy and Darnell had departed. My stomach tightened at the thought of being left alone with Shirley who now was starting to scare me more than Javier ever did. Her pleasant façade had disappeared as soon as the pinto turned the corner. I swallowed hard, trying to hold back tears as I peered into the sink full of dishes I was barely tall enough to reach.

The water was dirty and as I reached for the silverware toward the bottom, I found them slimy to the touch. My appetite vanished but I knew if I told Shirley that I had changed my mind about eating, it would only make her angry. There were some things my father taught me well. I found a dishrag and succeeded in washing out a bowl and spoon, poured myself a bowl of Froot Loops and sat quietly at the table.

After a few bites I found the fruity taste actually had somewhat begun to cheer me up or maybe I was just experiencing my first real sugar high. Nonetheless, I began to wonder about her girls. In this case I hoped the apple fell indeed, far from the tree. The clock on the wall read 1:37pm and although my brother and I had never attended a real school, I figured it wouldn't be too much longer before they arrived home. I thought back to the dolls and stuffed animals displayed in their room and how much fun it would be to have somewhat of a sister.

I cleaned out my dishes without any prompting, placed them in the rack next to the cluttered sink and returned to the living room. I watched the hands on the wall clock tick slowly, sure that the thing must be broken. There could be no way that a second should take so long. I counted one Mississippi, then two and so on. Trying to be as quiet as possible I started counting my breaths per minute then holding them as long as I could. I paid attention to the number of commercials that occupied slots between what seemed to be, to Shirley, a life or death daytime drama. After years of being alone with very little entertainment or amusement, I had taught myself simple and rather odd ways to keep my mind busy. Shirley remained on the couch, still biting her fingernails and paying me no mind.

Wondering if she was in the habit of taking in strange children with no place to call home, like an orphanage, I remembered Annie,

Heidi and all of the other storybook characters I had read about. Then I thought, with our situation, we more resembled Hansel and Gretel, yet that would make her the wicked witch and I shuddered at the thought. I peered toward the kitchen, sizing up the oven, and then shook my head dismissing the idea quickly. I missed my mother and my father. I even missed their arguments, the sound of their raised voices and the fear I often felt being caught in the middle, pretending to sleep through their spats.

I must have fallen back asleep for I awoke to the sound of the door opening. I was startled, completely forgetting about my new surroundings and from the seated position I was in, had assumed myself to be back in the rear seat of the Buick. My first instinct was to cry. I could feel the tears welling in my eyes but was distracted by the sounds of high pitched laughter. I glimpsed a ponytail, blondish in color disappear down the hall, and then watched it spin abruptly as the little girl turned, walked slowly back and took up position in front of me.

"Who are you?"

"My name is… is…" I couldn't remember who I was supposed to be. My voice caught in my throat as she peered down at me with piercing blue eyes.

"This is Bessie" Shirley chimed in to my relief, "She'll be staying with us for a while. This, is my daughter Bianca, she's the same age as you" she said bending to give her a kiss to which the little girl turned away her cheek, keeping her gaze directly on me.

"Are you black or Mexican" she questioned, frowning up her face and tilting her head to one side.

"Where is your sister?" Shirley asked her, buying me more time to gather my thoughts. Not that the second question was as challenging as the first but I was completely taken off guard by her abruptness.

"She comin', Mama! So what are you?"

"My Daddy is black and my Mama's white." This was the first of many times in my life I would offer this answer in explanation for my tan complexion and loose curls. Darnell, even though with lighter skin, had coarse hair and more predominantly black features, I had always been the odd one.

"Oh, so you a little half breed girl, I was gonna ask that myself, but she beat me to it." Shirley butt in again.

"Like that dog we had? Remember you said Coco was a half breed, Mama" Bianca turned to her mother, finally giving me a chance to exhale.

The door opened again then banged shut, blowing in a blast of wind from the force. An older girl walked through, throwing her backpack on the floor and stopping in her tracks at the sight of me. She looked almost exactly like her sister but had brown hair like her mother with matching eyes that didn't quite burn a hole right through me.

"Who is she, Mama?" She didn't bother to address me directly, looking me up and down with curiosity.

I hadn't had an opportunity to wash up or to change clothes, not that I had anything other than what currently adorned my body. I probably smelled and didn't even own a toothbrush. I closed my eyes, trying to envision myself anywhere but here. I could feel the stares from the three of them as they stood over me like giants, passing judgment from behind their frowning faces.

Shirley explained again to the oldest girl, Rosa, that I was a temporary guest. I studied the hole in my left sneaker intently, waiting for the next onslaught of questions that was headed my way.

"She's a half breed." Bianca told her sister "Like Coco, cause she ain't one thing or the other." She turned back to me "We used to call her a mutt. That's what they call dogs like that, you know. Where she gon' sleep, Mama?"

"She gon' sleep in y'all room, now hush with that nonsense. You want some new clothes for school, you just gon have to get used to it." Shirley didn't hold back in the least, apparently I was just a meal ticket or rather, a shopping spree.

"What's your name?" Rosa asked in a much gentler tone. I could tell she was quieter, subdued and hoped she would end up being my friend. Bianca was scowling, arms crossed and not willing to let me get a word in.

"Her name is Bessie and she's dirty. Mama, she stinks!"

"Bianca, go find some old clothes she can wear, she didn't come with nothin' and you're right, she sure need a bath." Shirley laughed, turning away from all of us and sauntered down the hall, leaving me to be gawked at like an animal in the zoo. Bianca followed like a puppy on her heels, continuing her insults.

"She can't sleep with us, there's no room! I'm not sharing a bed with her because she smells and why does she have to wear my clothes? That's not fair!"

I heard Shirley telling her as they continued further down the hall that I would sleep on the floor, not in her bed, but that it would be in her room. Rosa still remained in front of me, apparently curious but too shy to ask any questions. She opened her mouth as if to speak then decided against it, picking up her backpack and trailing after her mother. I lowered my head, folded my hands in my lap and could no longer contain the trembling in my lip. My tears fell silently and for that I was thankful. The last thing I wanted was to be labeled a cry baby and a stinky cry baby at that.

After a few minutes I heard Shirley calling out my name down the hall. I reluctantly obeyed, walking as slowly as possible, taking time to study the cracks in the walls and numerous spots on the brown carpet. I found her in the bathroom, running water that appeared to be entirely too hot, steam was rising and I could feel the heat as I approached the room. She had laid out a towel and what appeared to be a torn My Little Pony nightgown on top of the toilet seat.

"Go 'head, get in girl. You gotta get that funk off you."

I waited for her to leave and when she made no attempts to do so, continued to undress and stepped with one foot gingerly into the scalding water. It was just as I had suspected, way too hot. I jumped back splashing water on the floor and getting her purple muumuu wet in the process.

"Damn girl, whatcha do that for? Get in the water and stop playin around!"

I whimpered, but complied. My feet burned and seemed to be turning red on contact. I tried to remain standing as long as I could but she yanked my arm downward, forcing me to a sitting position. I tried again to stand up but her grip was firm and her expression let me know she was not a woman to be reckoned with. I began to cry, loudly this time and I swear I could hear snickering from behind the cracked door. I knew Bianca was there listening, enjoying every minute of my suffering.

She grabbed a washrag and started scrubbing my body, hard, leaving marks along my skin in the process from her bright red, dragon lady nails. I continued to cry but she paid me no mind nor did the hot bath give me any mercy. She washed my hair which was matted and tangled but didn't bother to comb it. The soap was getting in my eyes and I began to sob louder. I tried to wipe them but was met with resistance as her hands repeatedly shooed mine away from my face.

"There's soap in my eyes!" I cried out.

"Put your hands down, girl, and quit hollerin'. I'm almost done with you!"

Shirley dunked my head under to rinse my hair and I swallowed about half a cup of bathwater in the process. I sat up, choking and spitting, dangerously close to vomiting. She reached into the tub, pulled out the stopper then stood up, flinging a dry towel at me in disgust and left the room.

I jumped out of the bath as quickly as possible, my body shivering violently from the drastic change in temperature. I started to dry myself, seated on the side of the tub and watched the water swirl counter clockwise down the drain. Managing to rid my skin of most of the water but my hair held the rest like a sponge. I tried wrapping the towel around my head like a turban, the way my mother used to do with hers but kept failing miserably. I didn't want to leave the bathroom.

Rosa poked her head in the door after about ten minutes. The water had been long gone from the bathtub, leaving me staring at the light brown ring surrounding its edges. She entered, closing the door gently behind her and began to wash around the sides of the tub as best as she could with the washrag I had used.

"Are you okay?" she asked me.

I had been watching her, not thinking she would speak, wondering how she could be so opposite from her younger sibling whom apparently hated my guts for who knows what reason. I nodded my head, yes and simultaneously began to tear up again. She reached over and handed me the nightgown, motioning me to get dressed. I slid it over my small shoulders and inhaled the scent of what I thought was either detergent or fabric softener. It smelled good. Then I realized it was me.

It wasn't that I had never bathed before, my mother always made sure we were as clean as could be under the circumstances. It was just, more often than not, our showers consisted of washing up in gas station restrooms or restaurants where we stayed our nights hiding in back booths out of sight of management. This time was pleasant, not rushed and the soap smelled much better than whatever came out of those dispensers. If it had not been for the fact that my skin felt as if it were about to peel off from the scalding water and friction of

Shirley's poor bedside manner, I would have found it to be a completely enjoyable experience.

Rosa helped me to dry my hair and suddenly stopped. Placing her ear to the door she must have heard a commotion coming from down the hall, she handed me the towel and slipped out as quickly as she had come in. I was alone again but now felt, somehow through it all, I had a confidant. I sat again on the edge of the tub until I heard, what had become, my new name being called from elsewhere inside the house.

"Bessie, what you takin' so long for girl? C'mon out here, there's someone I want you to meet." Shirley's voice interrupted my daydream about flowers and friendship and I abided reluctantly. Hanging my towel on the rack and placing my clothes on top of the already full hamper, I headed back into the living room.

I smelled him before I saw him. His stench reached around the wall toward me, carrying with it a pint of liquor and a pack of cigarettes. His face half hidden by a thick black moustache and five o'clock shadow. The man was seated on the couch closest to me, hunched over, rolling a silver dollar repeatedly over his dirty knuckles. He looked up at me when I approached with beady, bloodshot eyes and I could feel my skin crawl from the roots of my hair down to my toes.

"Que Bonita" he slurred, "who is this?"

Shirley explained to him my circumstance in as much detail as she could while pouring him a drink from a bottle he apparently had provided her with. He never once took his eyes off me.

"This here… is the man of the house. Juan, this Bessie. She's, I guess you could say, our newest addition." Shirley took a seat next to him wrapping her arms around his neck and whispering something in his ear. I heard Leroy's name and then she pulled back, laughing. She grabbed the glass from him, took a drink and set it down on the table in front of them. I looked around for Rosa and Bianca, who were nowhere in sight.

"You want somethin' to eat, Papi?" she asked, leaning over him, rubbing his thigh. I had noticed she had changed out of her homely purple ensemble into a jean mini skirt that was begging for mercy and a pink tank top that showed off her more than ample cleavage. Her voice had taken on a much softer tone and any anger that she had toward me seemed to dissipate upon his arrival.

He shook his head from side to side, keeping me in his direct line of sight. Shirley shrugged her shoulders and went into the kitchen anyways. I could hear her running water and fumbling with the dishes in the sink. I remained standing in the doorway and must have been holding my breath for I was suddenly aware that I was light headed. My knees buckled slightly as he reached his grimy hand out to me.

"Venaqui, Mija" he beckoned me in his direction, patting the couch cushion next to him. "Come sit with me."

I stood frozen, feet glued to the floor with fright. I ended up being saved by my new worst enemy, I'm sure by default. Bianca came bouncing around the corner, ponytail swaying as if the room were filled with music, grinning from ear to ear.

"Papi" she squealed in delight, running and jumping into his lap as a dog would greet its master. I'm surprised she didn't lick him on the face. I almost smiled at the analogy. Yes, we both could play the canine reference game, I thought silently. The force in which she landed startled him, his face briefly displayed annoyance then shifted into a half smile. He wrapped his arms around her and kissed her on the cheek, his eyes still trained on me.

I wondered where Rosa was as I watched him playfully tickle her, whispering in her ear. He fetched a piece of hard candy from the pocket of his leather jacket and placed it in her hand. She was obviously his favorite and she would have no worries about me competing for his affection. I wanted to slip away but realized I had nowhere to go just yet. From overhearing Shirley's earlier conversation I knew I would end up on the floor of the girl's room but it was still early and there was still too much time to kill before the night came to an end.

Shirley appeared again in the living room, drying her hands on a towel. I could smell the aroma of food filling the house and my stomach began convincing me that I was again hungry though a series of grumbles and growls. The clock read 6:17pm. Juan had since turned his attention away from me back to his glass of liquor and the TV in front of him. Bianca sat curled into a small ball at his side.

"Rosa, come out here and help me with this food" she called.

Rosa appeared quickly from around the corner, brushing past where I stood, her eyes studying the floor. She didn't look at the dark haired man even once as she passed him by. I could feel the tension in the air, thicker than grits. She hurried to the kitchen and they both disappeared to finish preparing dinner. The table had been cleared of the remnants from the morning's meal and most of the stray items that had been covering the floor had been put away in their prospective places.

I finally mustered the nerve to take a seat on the couch, placing myself in as far proximity from Juan as possible. I caught Bianca intermittently casting her evil eye in my direction but pretended not to notice. The evening proceeded without incident. Shirley served us a meal of tacos and rice, which wasn't anything to write home about but I was, by no means, complaining. I had eaten three times that day which I felt sure, was a record.

Later on I had a chance to talk again with Rosa in private while Bianca was bathing. I learned she was ten years old and that Juan was neither her, nor her sister's biological father. She disclosed to me her dislike of him but was reluctant to go into any further detail.

Shirley made a palate of old blankets for me on the floor and gave me an old comforter to sleep with. This position placed me in close proximity to the lower bunk and far too close for comfort to where Bianca slept.

That night produced for me nightmares that were both extremely vivid, bordering on reality much more than I would have liked. I found myself back in the motel I had spent my first night, with Bianca spitting cockroaches from her mouth onto my naked body as I laid strapped to the bed, unable to move. Shirley and Juan stood laughing as they covered me from head to toe. I was screaming when I awoke.

I got up, walked into the living room, checking the wall clock on my way to the bathroom, 3:47am. It was destined to be a long night indeed. I heard arguing from behind the door of Shirley's bedroom and wasn't shocked. This was something I was used to although, in this case, most of the words were in Spanish. I went back to my room and lay down, waiting for morning to come. I was hoping Leroy would arrive early. I couldn't wait to see Darnell.

Shirley was shaking me. I opened my eyes, trying to adjust to the sunlight peering in from the window and my surroundings, simultaneously. I looked up at the bunk beds, they were empty. I could hear the girl's voices down the hall getting ready for school. It became apparent they were fighting over the toothpaste.

"Get up, you ain't sleepin' all day. You goin' to school with the girls." She stated, rummaging through dresser drawers, throwing clothes in my direction.

"But I thought my brother was coming with Leroy, he said they would come see me today." I objected, my voice still thick with sleep and rubbing my eyes.

"He can come back later if he misses you." She shot a stern look in my direction. "Put those on." She had tossed me a pair of faded jeans about two sizes two big and yellow tee shirt.

"But Miss Shirley, I wanna see my brother, please!" I started to cry. Not only did I miss Darnell tremendously but I was absolutely terrified of going to school.

"You're not staying here with me, now get dressed!"

She grabbed my arm, pulling me to my feet. I struggled, yanked away from her and in the process, tripped over the covers still on the floor and landed on my rear. She reached out again for me, this time grasping a fistful of my hair and shoved me toward the door.

"I said, get your ass dressed, now! Don't play wit' me girl, if you know what's good for you!"

Sniveling, I walked to the now vacant bathroom, carrying the clothes she had given me in one hand and wiping my tears with the other. I used the toilet and donned the outfit Shirley had picked out for me. I looked ridiculous but didn't care, the day couldn't get any worse and I had been awake for not even five minutes.

Rosa and Bianca were at the table eating cold cereal when I entered the room. They looked up at me with raised eyebrows then went back to their tasks at hand without saying a word. I sat in the available chair staring at the empty bowl that had been placed in front of me. Rosa pushed the box of Captain Crunch in my direction. I reached for the cereal, filling my bowl barely half way and poured the milk. Chewing slowly, I realized I had no appetite at all. I thought it ironic that for the first time in my life, I had what seemed to be an abundance of food at my fingertips only to find myself not hungry.

After finishing breakfast, I was instructed to put on my shoes and given an old backpack Shirley had found for my first day of school. I rode in the back seat of Shirley's red Toyota taking in the scenery which consisted of once brightly colored, but now faded homes and a small strip mall. The school loomed over us as we approached. It was built of gray concrete which resembled more of a correctional facility and was surrounded by a chain link fence much taller than I was.

Shirley parked in one of the spaces reserved for visitors and the girls jumped eagerly from the car and headed toward their classes. I didn't move. Shirley got out and adjusted her seat allowing me to crawl out of the small space and into the crisp but smoggy air. The smells were much different here. We walked up the wide cement steps to the double doors of what must have been the main office. I felt as if I was going to pee my pants.

The office smelled like books and was decorated with children's artwork from what I assumed were all different grades and ages. I admired the bright colors and simple shapes of those that belonged to the kindergarten classes and studied the intricacy of the ones obviously created by older children. The woman behind the front desk had white hair and a big smile. Her desk placard read Mrs. Hodges.

I remained quiet, taking in every detail of the building which was far opposite from the exterior. There were kids seated against the adjacent wall in wait, for what, I did not know. I listened to Shirley as she explained that I was her niece and would be staying with her family for a while so she would be enrolling me temporarily. Mrs. Hodges handed her a clipboard with a stack of papers and instructed us both to take a seat, winking at me from the corner of her eye. I pictured her as the grandmother I had never met.

Ironically, I had never met any of my family outside of my immediate household, so to speak. I had aunts and uncles on both my mother and fathers side but in the last two days had acquired one of each, unrelated by blood, and wasn't fond of either. I remained seated as Shirley returned the paperwork, flashed a fictitious smile in my direction and walked out the door. Mrs. Hodges came from around her desk with a folder apparently for me.

"Good morning, Bessie. Are you ready for your first day of school?" she asked, her tone sweet and sincere. "You will be in Ms.

Clark's first grade class. She is a wonderful teacher and will just love you to pieces! Let's get you set up, honey."

She called to another student, possibly a fourth grader, to escort me to room number B5. The boy was tall, lanky and had hair the color of cedar. He smelled like soap and didn't smile in the least. We walked in silence out the back door and into a large courtyard. I could hear the murmur of voices from open doors and could see student seated in desks with their hands raised, attentive. I wondered how I would fit in. I had never even set foot in a classroom before and didn't think I wasn't even old enough to attend school. I was more than thankful to my mother, now, for teaching me to read at such an early age.

I thought a saw a glimpse of Bianca as we passed one of the rooms on my right and was grateful I had not been placed in the same class as her. The boy stopped and stared at me. I realized we were in front of my classroom by reading the numbers positioned over the top of the blue metal door. I entered. The teacher had been made aware I was coming and greeted me warmly, showing me to a desk toward the back of the room. I could hear snickering from the children as I walked past.

"Ewww.... Look at her hair" Shirley had done absolutely nothing with it that morning and it remained matted and in disarray.

I looked around the room to see a variety of faces. Some of them black, some white but mostly Hispanic children. I took my seat and opened the folder I had been given by Mrs. Hodges, trying to avoid any eye contact with the other kids. The lesson plan that day consisted of spelling words that I already knew and I breathed a sigh of relief. I did not want to made fun of because I was ugly and stupid. At least I could keep up with the curriculum.

At recess I choose to stay in class. I didn't attempt to look for Rosa and was trying to avoid running into Bianca at any cost. At lunch, I took up residence at a table where no one else was sitting in the back of the cafeteria, the one closest to the trash vestibule. Apparently, Shirley had signed me up for the lunch program so I ate without charge. I wondered if Darnell had eaten this morning and more so, if he and Leroy had come by the house looking for me

When the dismissal bell rang I placed my folder in the backpack I had been given and wrestled with the broken zipper, hence the reason it was no longer being put to use. I followed the other children outside to the front of the school and tried to locate either of the girls amidst the mob of children hurrying to their destinations. I had no luck but did find Shirley parked along the sidewalk in her Celica smoking a cigarette, today she was wearing what looked like a turquoise muumuu.

I had mixed emotions as I approached the car. I was replaying over and over again my rude awakening but was looking forward to finding out if she had heard from Leroy and my brother. As I neared the vehicle I could see the scowl on her face. Balancing her cigarette in her mouth she gestured toward the backseat with her thumb, instructing me to get in.

"You find Rosa and Bianca?" the smoke swirled around her face in light gray wisps, the wind sending it looping around the bucket seats after me.

"No" I crept in behind the passenger seat, placing my backpack on the floor.

"Never mind, here they come. Scoot over so Bianca can fit."

I saw the girls walking up with a handful of their friends. Bianca pointed in my direction, giggling and whispered to a dark haired girl standing next to her. The girl's jaw dropped then she burst into a fit of uncontrollable laughter and headed in the other direction. She waved goodbye to the two of them and ran off to catch up to another crowd of kids that had gathered on the sidewalk. Bianca climbed in the car beside me.

"Move!" she said, setting her backpack on the seat between us, building a barrier.

Rosa turned around from the front seat offered me a shy smile then turned to look out the window for the remainder of the ride home. I didn't say a word the entire way to the house, deciding I would wait until Bianca wasn't around before asking about Darnell. Honestly, I was more worried about my next encounter with Juan, who gave me the creeps more than any man I had ever met. A little girls wrath was nothing compared to the fear I felt toward him.

When we arrived, there was a big truck parked in front but no pinto. I hung my head, dragging my feet all the way to the front door. Shirley headed immediately to the kitchen, grabbed the phone from the wall to place a call, stretching the cord all the way to the couch. I heard her ask for Leroy and assumed she was speaking with Javier, the hotel manager. Amazingly, I felt a pang of sorrow. I would have much rather been in his company than here, sans the cockroaches, of course.

My hopes perked up with the realization that I hadn't missed them. I would still have a chance to see Darnell. A man with my color complexion appeared in the hallway. He wore a white tank top, dark blue Levi's and his light brown hair in an afro surrounding his face, accentuated with a black pick.

"Uncle Jesse!" the girls squealed simultaneously. He scooped them both up in his arms at the same time, his laughter soft and soothing.

"Yo Mama tells me y'all got a houseguest. This da little girl right here?" He said looking at me.

"Yeah" Bianca replied "She don't talk much."

He placed the two of them back on solid ground and headed toward me with his arm extended, palm facing up. I shook it awkwardly.

"You can call me Uncle Jesse, and I don't bite like the rest of 'em around here" he joked.

"You better bring me my fuckin' money Leroy, I'll put her ass out, she already givin' me problems." Shirley stormed again into the kitchen. I heard the phone slam onto the receiver and cringed.

"Aww, don't pay her no mind, so Leroy brought ya over here, huh? I ain't seen my man in a long time."

I didn't know what was going on but I knew I didn't want to be "put out" especially without Darnell and sincerely hoped Leroy would pull through with whatever his end of bargain was. Plus, the more upset she was with the situation meant the more upset she would be with me.

Jesse popped in and out throughout the day and we girls played outside for the remainder of the afternoon. I learned the hard way that I was a terrible tetherball player. I think I ended up hitting the ball more times with my face than fists which, of course, had Bianca in stitches. Leroy and Darnell showed around seven o'clock.

I ran to my brother, hugging him so tight he was gasping for breath and trying to pry himself out of my embrace. He looked down at me with a smile but there was something much more somber behind the brown of his eyes, almost a twinge of guilt. His pea coat smelled like cigarette smoke and sweat.

"Hey sis" his voice was depleted of any joy "how are things going?"

Everything came out in a rush. I told him about the girls and my first day of school, being careful of my phrases as we had an audience. I pulled him toward the couch to sit down but he resisted.

"Leroy said we can't stay long." He bent down to whisper in my ear "are they treating you okay?"

My eyes filled with tears. I couldn't tell him about the way Shirley had snatched me by my hair just this morning or about the uneasy feeling I had about the man who spent the night. Shirley was eyeballing me with a scowl even now as she stood in the kitchen counting out the bills Leroy had given her. I nodded my head.

"Look sis, I might not be able to come back for a few days, I need you to be strong for me. We're gonna be alright. I'm trying to find a way that you can come and stay with me. Remember this is just temporary. Keep your head up and don't cry, okay?"

"Baby girl" Leroy shouted, coming up behind me and slapping me on the back. I turned and scrunched up my nose as his breath reeked of garlic and cigarettes. He was dressed in blue jeans and a brown ribbed turtleneck complete with matching fedora. His eyes were hidden behind the same dark pair of shades he had worn the first day I met him.

I looked past his slender frame and out the open doorway to where night had begun to fall, casting shadows over the city. I could make out the silhouette of a woman positioned in the front seat of the pinto, judging by the size and shape of her blonde hair, I assumed it to be Candy. I wondered if Leroy's brother was ever going to get his car back.

I had always been caught up in fairy tales, wishing for the impossible. So here I was, hoping that one day like Dorothy perhaps, I could with three clicks of my heels awake to find myself in the back seat of the Buick I called home. There were no words Darnell could utter that would console me. My sobs increased in volume and drew the attention of all within earshot. Jesse appeared from the hallway with a puzzled look on his face and my brother stood looking down at me helpless.

He wrapped his arms around me, pulling my small body into his chest. I could feel deep in my bones that he was right and that the time before I would see him next would be far longer than even he expected. I knew Shirley and her daughters didn't care about my well being. I was nothing to them and that any displeasure on my part was to her girls, Bianca at least, a mere form of entertainment.

"What's with the waterworks?" Jesse stood looking dumbfounded.

"What's goin' on, Jesse? She be alright, you know girls." Leroy answered his question, rolling his eyes and jingling his keys in his right hand. "Shirley, you good with that?"

My tormenter nodded from the space adjoining the kitchen and living room, leaning up again the wall and fingering her newly acquired wad of cash.

"No problems here."

"C'mon Johnny, wrap it up. We got places to be and people to see." He tousled my hair, gave Darnell an impatient look and sauntered out the door.

Darnell grabbed both of my shoulders, stooping down to kiss me on my forehead and whisper in my ear.

"I'm sorry, sis."

He didn't bother looking back. He didn't bother saying goodbye. Maybe it hurt him too much to leave but I knew as well as he did that he had no choice. My nose was running and my eyes were producing tears like a saltwater stream. I sniveled, wiping the snot from my chin with the back of my hand and thought again of my mother.

I heard the commotion behind me, the girls squabbling over maybe perhaps a toy of some sort. I drowned out the sounds of their bickering, my feet were stuck to the floor and my eyes focused only on the two figures becoming proportionately smaller as they gained distance. I heard the start of the pinto's engine; the sound was muffled in my head as I was in a fog of denial. I would be alone with these strange people for an undetermined amount of time and I knew it would not be to my benefit.

The next few weeks were monotonous. I learned to deal with my situation by staying out of the way. I found a stack of books packed in a box in the far corner of the girl's closet that kept me company, allowing me to be a rebel and a heroine within their pages. Bianca maintained her attitude with no attempt to hide her dislike of me and I leaned that Rosa's kindness was only short lived though she never ended up being as much of a tyrant as her sister.

Shirley's house seemed to apparently have a revolving door. I would often awake in the middle of the night to the smell of smoke and the sound of raucous laughter belonging to a plethora of different voices. I had no idea what it was they were doing and never had the desire to find out. In daylight hours, I had become accustomed to being introduced as the niece from out of town. No questions asked.

I came to know Shirley as an alcoholic. This was figured out between her fits of screaming and uncontrollable crying which took place at all hours of the day with liquor bottles in hand. She made no attempts to hide it, often asking her daughters or myself to fetch or pour one glass after another. She had a tendency of falling asleep or rather passing out on the couch, lit cigarette still in hand. How the house never burned down is a mystery to me.

The only time I saw the woman happy was in Juan's presence which was a catch 22. Even though I was glad for her smiles instead of scowls I couldn't stand the man. Being in his proximity sent chills up my spine and though their days were spent with laughter their nights almost always ended in fights.

I awoke to a loud bang coming from either the kitchen or living room, I couldn't tell which. I looked up at the girls bunks and if they had heard it, they pretended that they didn't, neither of them moved. I heard Shirley's raised voice, she was cursing like a sailor and sounded near tears, another bang. The door to the room was cracked and I could see a sliver of light peeking in.

I stood up wrapping my comforter around me and walked slowly to the door, pulling it open just a tad more. I poked my head into the hallway but could see nothing. I crept quietly down the hall standing on the other side of the wall and took a deep breath. It was a love and hate relationship that I had with my own curiosity. My head popped around the corner for just an instant and that was all it took.

In that single moment the sight I beheld frightened me so much I couldn't move my feet. Shirley was standing in the middle of the living room, stark naked. Her pale body was covered in cellulite from head to toe and her midsection contained rolls that hung over and rested on her thighs. She stood holding a raised frying pan in her hand and was now screaming at the top of her lungs. Her cheeks were streaked with mascara, lipstick smeared down her chin and the large mass of hair which once framed her round face was gone. She was completely bald.

I began to feel lightheaded and realized I was holding my breath. I exhaled just as I caught Juan standing in the corner of the living room, yet he wasn't looking at Shirley, who at this time was giving him her full attention and apparently a piece of her mind. He was staring directly at me, smiling. I gasped, covering my mouth to stifle the sound and turned on my heels, running at breakneck speed back to the bedroom. I made sure to close the door quietly to not draw any further attention and lay back on the floor. I was waiting to hear the creaking of the door or footsteps down the hall but they never came.

The next morning, things had returned to normal. I awoke to find Shirley on the couch absorbed in a TV program with a full head of hair. She looked at me with a smug expression but nothing to give way the fact that she knew last night I had been watching her. I stared at her and she returned my gaze with mutual hatred, nothing new there. She wore a wig, I figured out, trying to keep from studying her hairline I tore my eyes away and continued to get ready for school.

The girls had me at their discretion or should I say at their beck and call. I was afraid of Shirley and they both knew it, using it to their advantage to get me to finish their chores, make their food and basically play the fool for them. They would often wake me up in the middle of the night to play house, doctor or school until the sun would rise and they would sneak off to bed so as not to get caught. I was always made to play the role of the dumb student being sent to a makeshift principal's office which meant being forced to stand in the corner until my legs would almost give way. I would on more than one occasion, fall asleep as I was dressing one doll or another, awaking to Bianca pinching me repeatedly until I did her bidding.

I ended up being blamed for everything from broken dishes and unlocked doors to missing jewelry. The girls threw me under the bus almost daily and I learned that Shirley could swing a belt with the best of them. Growing up with my father, I was used to getting whippings but not without at least a little love behind them. I learned that in punishment, that does make a difference, as odd as it seems. There were times I thought the woman would kill me.

My nightmares were horrendous and too often included tragedy and death. Darnell's face appeared more than I would have liked and I would awake in a cold sweat with tears in my eyes. Rosa complained to her mother that she couldn't sleep with me screaming so on many nights I would be forced to lie at the foot of Shirley's bed, wrapped in a small comforter and my own fear.

It had been at least six weeks since I had seen my brother so when the phone rang and Shirley called me in the kitchen, I was doing cartwheels mentally and the smile on my face was as wide as the Mississippi River. Shirley handed me the receiver reluctantly not concerned with my happiness so much as when she would be receiving her next installment payment. I was beyond giddy, stretching the cord to its distance and curling it around my fingers, taking a seat on the linoleum in the corner. I placed my back against the refrigerator, as far out of earshot as possible.

"Darnell…is it you?" I asked. My tone was barely above a whisper.

"Yeah, sis" his voice was muffled by background noise and he sounded tired, worn out. "Are you okay?"

"Yes, but I want to go home. Why haven't you come to see me?"

"Leroy's had me doin' a lot of stuff for him and he just gave me the phone number there. I'm coming this weekend. Are they being nice to you?"

"Well," I hesitated answering, I didn't want him to worry "They're not as nice as I thought they were gonna be and I miss you. I'm scared Darnell and I want to see Mom. I want to go home"

"Anna, I told you we can't go home," his voice cracked on the other end of the line "I'll see you Friday, don't worry, I'll figure something out."

There was a click followed by the dial tone and I sat there, looking at the receiver until it began a series of beeping sounds. I slowly got to my feet and placed it back on its base that hung on off white wall stained with the remnants of food and fingerprints. He would be here in five days.

Jesse walked in the front door carrying a twelve pack of beer in his left hand and a large brown paper bag in his right. Shirley met him in the entryway relieving him of his package and began rummaging through its contents. She pulled out two bottles of brown liquor setting them on the counter next to the half-eaten bowls of cereal left from this morning's breakfast.

"Bessie, get back in here and clean up these dishes girl!"

I could hear Rosa and Bianca playing outside, the pang of the tether ball wrapping around the steel pole, their laughter chiming over that of the other neighborhood kids who had come to join in. I wasn't upset over not being included and honestly had stayed inside by choice. I avoided them as much as possible, especially at school. I had no desire to be the butt of their jokes and whenever they were amongst their friends their hatred for me seemed to amplify.

What had begun to wear on me was the fact that I had become a modern day Cinderella. I had read enough fairy tales to know that there was always a happy ending but for me, there was no Prince Charming in sight. The girls would leave clothes around the house, dirty dishes on the table and even though Shirley knew the fault was not mine, I was expected to clean up their mess. She would often bring them gifts, candy, dolls and little knick knacks when all I received were her sour expressions.

Bianca would rub it in every chance she got, even going as far as to ask me if I wanted to play with her newly acquired toys then telling Shirley I had taken them from her. I wanted out, any way possible. I even considered running away on my own but the thought of Darnell never being able to find me kept me in place. Even though she was smaller than me, Bianca would bully me unmercifully. She pulled my hair, pinched and scratched me when no one was looking. Daring me to tell on her and laughing because she knew no one would believe me, or at least care enough to take action.

That morning Jesse announced that he was taking the girls to the movies. I paid him no attention, used to being left out of their activities so even though I had never been to a real movie theatre and desperately wanted to go, I pushed the thought far from my mind. Five days to go I told myself. I washed the last dish, placing it carefully in the rack and dried my hands. When I turned around, Shirley was there blocking my way with her arms crossed, tapping her foot.

"Well, what are you waitin' for? Put your shoes on.

"For what?" I asked.

"If you want to go with Jesse, you better hurry, ain't nobody waitin' on you"

I ran into the bedroom as fast as I could. I found one shoe in the closet, right where it should be but couldn't locate the other. I could feel the tears welling in my eyes as I searched under the bed, the dresser and everywhere I could think it might have been. I heard snickering and turned to see Bianca holding my matching shoe in her hand. She threw it at me laughing and headed out of the room.

"Uncle Jesse, wait for me" she called out, running down the hall, still giggling.

Jesse drove an old, rusted cobalt blue truck that seated only three in the front. I sat behind the cab portion, in the bed of the pickup as he drove like a mad man through the streets of Los Angeles. I swear he hit every bump possible and by the time we reached our destination, my rear end was sore and I was almost in tears. The sight of the movie theatre took my mind off the pain. It was huge. The marquee was brightly lit and there were people everywhere. The smell of popcorn filled the air even in the entryway and I was completely in awe at the vastness of its size and décor.

We approached the ticket window and I couldn't keep my eyes focused on any one thing. It was to me, glamorous, with velvet curtains hanging from the walls and floor length posters of upcoming features lining the interior. He told us to wait over by the arcade while he purchased our tickets. I stood with the girls who were excited but not nearly as much as I. Apparently they had been around this block a couple times before. Jesse returned waving our tickets in his hand and we followed him down a dark hall into one of the theatres on the right. I glanced at the sign above us that read, in bold capital letters, Children of the Corn.

I looked at the movie poster that mimicked the same title, its background blood red with a silhouette of a hand holding a scythe intended to strike. What or who, I didn't want to find out. I felt my heart skip a beat and begin to pound so furiously I was afraid it could no longer be contained within my chest. The lump that had started to grow in my throat doubled in size and my legs grew heavy as we approached the large double doors in front of us. I tugged on Jesse's sleeve.

"Uncle Jesse, I don't wanna go in there." I whispered.

He laughed, taking my hand and pulling me along. I tried to hold back, to resist his lead but his grip was firm and my strength no match for that of a grown man. I surrendered, walking with my head held low, blinking back tears. Rosa and Bianca pointed and giggled, they were having a field day with this one. As we took our seats, I found myself wedged between Rosa and Jesse, Bianca had gotten up and switched seats in order to not be in my close proximity. I had learned recently that cooties were contagious.

I had never seen anything like it. The screen was gigantic and the sound inside the theatre was thunderous. I was torn between awe and fear as I took in my surroundings. The movie began and I tried to cover my eyes to keep from looking but curiosity was getting the best of me and there was no way to block out the sound. Children lined up eerily as they succeeded in violently offing all the adults in the shabby little town. Amazingly amidst all of the bloodshed, the one thing that scared me the most and had all the hair on my body standing on end was their fingernails being a dark shade of blue. The sight of those little hands would haunt me for years to come.

By the time we left the theatre the sun had set and night caressed the city like a blanket. The wind in the back of the truck whipped at my face with a fierceness and shadows seemed not only to loom over but to follow us as we headed home. I could hear the three of them laughing in the front seat through the crack in the sliding window and was pretty sure it was at my expense.

When we got back to the house, we found Shirley passed out on the couch. Her cigarette which had been left to burn down to the butt teetered on the side of the circular glass astray. Yet another close call. One of the bottles of liquor remained on the table in front of her, half empty with no glass in sight. She was obviously not a classy drunk.

The girls ran off to their room, shrieking in the dark. I followed behind passing the doorway headed into the bathroom. After finishing my business I exited the bathroom to find both of them waiting for me outside in the hall.

"Are you still scared Bessie?" Bianca asked "Creeped out about their nails, huh? I heard you over there about to cry from two seats over!"

"Does she know about Bloody Mary?

"Who is Bloody Mary?" I piped up, wishing I wouldn't keep falling for their pranks but I did every single time.

"Come here and we'll tell you." Rosa pulled me into their dark room with Bianca following shutting the door behind her.

The curtain on the only window was drawn and the room was therefore pitch black. I stumbled over something on the floor but couldn't tell from the size or shape what it was. I could hear them talking back and forth between each other in hushed voices but couldn't see enough to make out their silhouettes or determine their whereabouts.

"She's a witch and she comes to kill you in the dark" Bianca whispered, apparently she was a lot closer than I had thought and I could feel her hot breath on my ear.

"If you spin around and say her name three times in the dark in front of a mirror, they say she will appear and scratch your eyes out." Rosa explained slowly, trying to maintain her mysterious façade "she's covered from head to toe in blood and you'll like this... she has long fingernails like knives" they both simultaneously burst into laughter.

"C'mon, let's try it." Bianca grabbed me by the arm, leading me back down the hall to the bathroom.

"No" I protested feet dragging my feet along the carpet. Rosa took my other arm. They are both crazy I thought. I had definitely seen enough blood for the day and was already traumatized. I began to cry.

"No, stop!" I yelled, hopping Shirley or Jesse would show up to prevent them from dragging me to death by witch. No such luck.

We reached the bathroom and they pushed me in first, locking the door behind them.

"Ready?" Rosa turned off the light.

"Let me out" I tried to get past her to no avail. She was both bigger and stronger than me, not to mention determined.

They pinned my arms to my side.

"Say it" Bianca whispered.

"No"

"Say it"

"No, let me go" I wriggled, trying to break free of their grasp. I couldn't see a thing. There wasn't a single window in the bathroom, not even any light from the hallway to creep under the door.

"Fine then, we will for you." Bianca said, I could tell the smirk was there, whether visible or not.

They began to turn me.

"Bloody Mary" they chimed at the same time.

My heart began to race faster than I could have ever imagined and I could feel the blood rushing through my ears. The tears rolled down my face without direction, flowing and I felt as though I couldn't breathe. I couldn't decide whether to keep my eyes open or closed. I tried to fight against them but nothing was working. The first turn was complete.

"Bloody Mary"

This time they spun me slower or maybe it was just my imagination. Their voices seemed to mimic that of a record player on slow speed.

This was the final turn, I had counted two already. I dreaded the words.

"Bloody Mary" they opened the bathroom door and exited quick as lightning, slamming it shut behind them.

I tried the knob, turning it from left to right but was met with resistance. It wouldn't budge. They were holding it tight from the other side. I heard them trying to stifle their giggles.

"Shhhh" one of them uttered and then all was silent.

I jiggled the handle then pulled it hard but it still wouldn't give way. I realized my eyes were still closed and for now there was no way out. There was a rustling in the room, coming from what I thought was the bathtub but I had lost my perspective with being spun around and the blackness suffocating the small area. I flung my eyes open but couldn't see a thing. Something was in here with me.

I felt the hands reach for me, the fabric of the shower curtain as it engulfed me. I screamed as the figure clawed upward at my face. I covered my eyes turning to run but tripped over the laundry hamper and fell clumsily to the floor. Scooting back on my behind I stretched my arms out trying to fend off whatever entity was after me. My hands connected with nothing but thin air when I heard it, low at first then its tone rising to a shrieking wail. I felt the strong fingers gripping my ankles and pulling me across the floor with what seemed to be a super human force.

The light blinded me. It took time for my eyes to adjust and in the interim the only sound filling my ears was a loud ringing noise. Maybe she got me. All five or seven years of my life, honestly I was confusing myself these days, flashed before my eyes. I had died and gone to heaven. Slowly my vision cleared and I looked up from my vantage point, wedged between the toilet seat and vanity, to see the faces of Rosa and Bianca in the doorway. In the middle of the floor and on his hands and knees was Jesse, doubling over with laughter. I thought it could only be children who were this cruel.

I fled the room, tears streaming down my face, snot pouring from my nose and ran smack dab into Shirley. My little body connected with her midsection like a brick wall as she blocked my path.

"What the hell is going on? What you screamin' for? Damn, I can't even get any fuckin' sleep in here!"

"Aww, we just playin' wit her Shirley, sorry to wake you up." Jesse walked past me "Movie was great, right girls?"

Rosa and Bianca nodded as they followed him into the living room and plopped down on the couch that had not been occupied by their mother, still snickering. I headed into their room and cried myself to sleep on the floor only to be awakened by Bianca within the hour.

"Get out. Mama said you have to sleep in her room tonight."

I grabbed my comforter, headed to the foot of Shirley's bed, curled up and again shut my eyes.

The weekend came and then went. I spent both consecutive days with my head glued to the pane of the front window looking for any sign of the green pinto. By Sunday morning I still hadn't heard from Darnell. He called that night. Shirley handed me the phone after what was a long heated conversation with whom, I assume, was Leroy.

"What do you mean you can't come?" I whined into the receiver.

"Leroy gave the car back and he said has to wait to get a ride to take me over there. I can't walk, Anna, it's too far."

"That's not fair! You told me you were coming" I had begun to cry again. Finally he had returned the car to his stinkin' brother, now this meant I couldn't see mine.

"He said he has to bring Shirley more money so we will be there soon, I promise, I just don't know when."

"Get off that phone, girl! I need to make a call" Shirley yelled at me from the living room.

"Shirley says I have to hang up, please come Darnell." I placed the receiver back on its cradle and went back to the girl's room. Bianca was outside playing but I still wouldn't risk sitting on her bed. I sat in the corner, placed my head between my knees and cried.

Juan usually came and went like a thief in the night. Shirley had once told me he was her husband but by the infrequency of his visits, I had begun to doubt it. I knew of his presence by his raised voice and Spanish dialect which often woke me in the wee hours of the morning. When he would appear during daytime I would try to stay in Rosa and Bianca's room and out of sight. He always looked at me oddly with his red beady eyes and gave me the willies.

He had been around a lot more frequently and on more than one occasion asked me to come and sit on his lap. Each time, if within earshot, Shirley would snap her head my direction and give me the evil eye. Luckily, I would often be saved by Bianca who would come into the room swinging her blond ponytail in full force and distract his attention. The girl was at least good for something.

Her birthday was coming and it was all I had heard about for the last three days. What new dolls she wanted, the tea set with an eight piece setting and a new purple bike. I was pretty sure she would get all of it. She bragged day and night to me about how many presents she got each year and how big her cake was. Her mother was planning a slumber party for her and she made it well known that I would not be invited. I didn't figure how well that would work as I was in the same household but where there was Bianca's will, there was always a way.

The party was on a Saturday and unfortunately found me in attendance. Her piñata was as big as she was, shaped like a pink pony. She wore her hair in braids and was fitted in a new pink frilly dress. There must have been thirty or more people filling the house and we had spent all Friday cleaning. The place wasn't quite spotless but it was as good as it was going to get. I was exhausted and all I wanted to do was sleep.

Most of the games we played were familiar to me but some not so much. I was called up to play what they referred to as a "rope game" which consisted of exactly that, a rope but also a blow pop. The sucker was to be tied in the middle with almost two feet of rope on each opposing end. The object was for each child to put the rope in their mouth as quickly as possible and the one to reach the candy first would win.

It was by far the stupidest and more disgusting thing I had ever heard of and I immediately said that I didn't want to participate.

"You have to" Bianca stated, apparently with her big mouth, she must have been a pro at this. "Mama, she said she won't play."

"Yes she will, Baby." Shirley shot me a sideways glance and continued her conversation with two of the guests.

"See, Mama said you will. Now, go over on that end."

I stood there holding the end of the coarse yellow rope between my fingertips, rolling it back and forth. It looked dirty and had obviously been used elsewhere for other feats much greater and more necessary than this. I couldn't believe this was meant to be fun or that the adults in the household approved. I glanced around at the other guests and met their eyes with looks of impatience.

"Go ahead, put it in your mouth and try to get to the middle, I'm gonna win anyways." Bianca actually had the audacity to brag about her pending triumph.

I did as was instructed and on the count of three, we both began. The rope tasted like soil and its fibers scratched the roof of my mouth. I immediately began to gag. As more of it entered, reaching the back of my throat, my eyes began to water. This was by no means my definition of a party game and though I hadn't been to any parties, period, I was sure this was not a commonplace procedure. I felt the bile rise up from my throat and looked through teary eyes at

Bianca who was nearing the sucker in the middle. I felt a pang of relief. It would be over soon.

She spit the rope out, wet with saliva, and it landed on the floor. She let out a cry of victory as I let it fall out of my mouth slowly. These people had a warped sense of entertainment. I ran immediately to the bathroom and began heaving over the commode. I was hoping Rosa's birthday was many, many months away and had decided, in that moment, to never disclose my date of birth. If asked, it would have been a year from yesterday.

The other festivities included the usual pin the tail on the donkey, musical chairs which I thought were fun but Bianca always cheated. Nothing new to me, I was used to her getting her way by any means necessary. I was only thinking about Darnell anyways and oddly enough, my father. Amazing how I had thought him to be the tyrant of all tyrants, the devil in disguise and now I found myself missing him. Remembering the way we would sing along to oldies and dance like no one was watching.

The party commenced and I grew tired, barely able to keep my eyes open, I succeeded in sneaking off to nap alongside Bianca's bed until I would soon be asked to move. I had already been informed that I would be sleeping in Shirley's room as Bianca's company would be staying the night. To that private party, I was not invited. Juan had been eyeballing me all day and I awoke to find him in the doorway looking down at me smiling.

"Mija, Mama say go to her room, it's late. You want Juan help you?" his English was broken, and his voice slurred from consuming an abundance of alcoholic beverages. I could smell it from across the room.

I shook my head no and sat up, clutching the comforter in my hands. He didn't move and neither did I. I suppose this was what they call a Mexican standoff. I would have to get undressed and put on my nightgown and he knew it. I could hear laughter from the living room and saw past him as two girls ran down the hall headed toward the bathroom. Shirley called his name. He clucked his tongue and shook his head at me, turning and closing the door behind him.

I put on my nightclothes and waited until I heard the girls coming down the hall to make my exit, comforter in tow. Shirley's room was dark and cluttered with bags and boxes left over from the plethora of gifts Bianca had received for this her eighth birthday. I scooted them over as much as possible and created a small space for myself, falling immediately back to sleep.

I heard the door creaking and with the moonlight peering through the thin curtains, could see a shadow enter the room. The aroma of liquor and stale cigarettes filled my nostrils and I froze. It could have been Shirley but my sixth sense told me otherwise. I could make out heavy breathing amongst the silence and knew it was him.

Everything seemed to proceed in slow motion. I watched his silhouette as he unbuttoned his shirt and saw his arms rise over his head as he removed his undershirt. Maybe he had forgotten I was in the room, I tried to reason with myself. He unfastened his belt buckle cursing under his breath as he stepped on the remnants of packaging strewn across the floor. I held my breath and a tear rolled slowly down my cheek. Where was Shirley?

I never missed the woman since I had met her. I prayed she was already in the room but couldn't feel her presence or warmth in the bed with me. He approached, running his hands over the covers, searching. The bed groaned as he placed his weight upon it, still groping. His touch was cold and clammy as the tips of his fingers connected with my leg. It took all I had not to move, hoping if I feigned sleep he would leave me alone.

The pace of his breathing increased as he began to stroke my knee. I whimpered unable to control my fear.

"Ah mija, you are awake." His voice was thick and husky. "Let me touch, I won't hurt you."

I pulled my leg away and within an instant he was beside me, his breath heavy in my ear.

"I want show you something but you no tell." He grabbed at me under my cover. I could feel his naked body beside me and begin to cry. I tried to get up but he pulled me back down, holding me tight.

"If you wake Mama she will be mad" he whispered "I tell her you are bad girl and she will beat you, no?"

He pulled me close to him, grabbing my hands so I couldn't move and then lifted them to his face, placing my fingers in his mouth. His moustache was coarse and scratched against my skin, his mouth was hot and wet and I could feel his tongue moving across my fingertips.

"Now you."

Still holding both of my hands within one of his, he tried to pry my mouth open with his free hand but my lips were pursed tight. He licked my face. I gasped and he shoved two of his fingers in my mouth. They tasted like dirt and salt, I gagged.

"You will like, Mija, I promise."

He guided my hands down the length of his hairy stomach until I felt something hard and he moaned. I yanked my hands away as quick as I could and started to cry louder.

"No, let me go." I yelled.

"Shut up!" His breathing was fast and his tone harsh, "touch it."

I was too afraid to speak but vigorously shook my head, no.

"Touch it"

He pulled my hand back down with force and rubbed it along the length of his penis. I grew lightheaded and realized I was starting to hyperventilate. The tears were flowing hard. He pushed my head down.

"Now kiss."

He grabbed a fistful of my hair and held me under the covers and began gyrating his body. The thing was touching my face and I felt vomit rise in my throat.

"Open your mouth"

I clenched my teeth shut, lips sealed.

He pulled me out from under the covers and threw me on the bed, sitting on top of me. My chest felt as if it would cave under his weight. He pried my mouth open with his fingers, scratching my gums with his nails, I tasted blood and he shoved his penis inside. I gagged and spit, thrashing my head from side to side and tried to scream. He withdrew his manhood and covered my nose and mouth simultaneously.

"Shut up! Shut up!" He yelled under his breath, eyes focused on the door.

I tried to crane my head backwards to see of someone was coming but was held fast to the bed. I was starting to see spots before my eyes and I couldn't breathe. He was going to kill me.

He released his grip and leaned down to whisper in my ear. "Shut up or I beat you myself."

I remained still, trying to control my sobs and for a minute he didn't touch me. I thought of getting up and running from the room but knew I wouldn't be fast enough to escape. Even in his drunken state, Juan still had the upper hand.

I felt him reaching under the comforter again, trying to pry my legs open. I held my knees together as tight as I could. He muttered something in Spanish then began to rub between my legs anyway, his nails scraping my skin.

"No!!!!" I yelled. I didn't care anymore whether Shirley beat me or he did.

He slapped me across my face, hard, then got up putting on his pants and shirt and left the room. I remained in the same position, unable to move, dreading his return. I cried until the sun came up.

When Shirley came in the morning she found my eyes bloodshot and my face streaked with tears. She looked at me and laughed.

"Nightmares again? Go clean yourself up."

I didn't answer her. I walked to the bathroom, pulled down my underwear and sat down on the toilet seat. There were bruises and scratch marks from where Juan had broken the skin trying to open my legs and my mouth was sore from the force of his hands. I didn't want to leave the bathroom. I didn't understand what happened or why it happened, I just knew it shouldn't have. Letting the water run in the sink I stared at myself in the mirror and began to cry again. I washed my face but the tears kept flowing.

There were no marks from where he had slapped me but my lips looked slightly swollen. I didn't think anyone would notice as they paid me no attention anyway. Shirley banged on the door and yelled for me to hurry up. I dried my face with a towel and wondered if he was still out there. I wanted to tell Darnell but somehow knew I couldn't. The words would never find their way out no matter how hard I tried.

I was ashamed and replayed the scenario over and over again in my mind, torturing myself repeatedly. I thought I should have fought harder. I should have screamed louder, no matter the consequence. I had allowed this to happen. If only I had run out of the room when I heard him undressing he would have never been able to touch me in the first place.

I banged my head against a brick wall metaphorically. If I ever did muster the courage to tell Darnell, what would he think of me? He would ask me why I didn't run, scream bloody murder. He would think I was a coward and didn't have the courage to fight back. The sister he knew would have put up a fight, he would have if he had been in that situation. I made up my mind. I would never let my brother know what happened that night.

I flushed the toilet and turned off the light, headed down the hall to the girl's room and peeked in. Blankets, pillows and little girls were still sprawled all over the floor. I closed the door and walked slowly back to Shirley's room, the last place I wanted to be. She was inside cleaning so I remained standing in the hall for a good five minutes for fear that he would be in the living room.

"What you doin' standing there?" Shirley asked me as she passed by carrying a handful of trash to the kitchen.

I shrugged my shoulders, unable to find my voice for fear of bursting into tears.

"Go in there and start picking up, the girls gonna be awake soon." She ordered, nodding toward the front room and rolling her eyes at me.

I wanted to ask if he was out there but I didn't dare speak his name as if summoning the devil. I remained in place.

"What's wrong wit you, girl? You lost your damn mind?" she approached quicker than I expected and shoved me out of the hall and into the living room with her spare hand. I stumbled as my body fell around the corner, hitting my knee on the side of the couch as I slumped to the ground.

I looked around wildly, my eyes huge and filled with terror. Gasping for air, not from the force she bestowed when physically removing me from my stance against the wall but from holding my breath in fear. He wasn't there. I stood up and walked slowly to the kitchen, Shirley studying my every move certain I had gone insane. In a way she was right, I had been broken in a way she never suspected.

The kitchen was empty with the exception of trash piled up in every corner but no physical presence. There were styrofoam plates stacked on every surface, spilling out of the garbage can and flies converging around the remnants of food left on the counters. The cake or what was left of it remained uncovered on the dining table. I began to gather the items, placing any actual dishes in the sink and listening intently for the sound of the front door.

The girls had awoken and the house was again instantly filled with laughter. My heart remained in the pit of my stomach. This day I had no objection to the abundance of chores. I cleaned the girl's room without asking, picking up bits and pieces of wrapping paper and torn packaging that was strewn across the floor and made myself as scarce as possible. I tried to hold back the tears that welled to no success. Rosa and Bianca gave me curios glances but chose to leave me alone. They had no idea what had transpired through the night but apparently had decided to focus their attention elsewhere.

The following days and nights blurred together through my intermittent tears. School became monotonous and any hope I had of seeing my parents again had diminished. I awoke crying on much more than one occasion with the fear that I would forget my mother's face. Juan showed less frequently in the coming weeks and always in the evening hours, after the girls and I had turned in for the night. I could sense his presence through the walls and my stomach would churn with fear. I began to sleep and eat less and any weight I had gained in the last few months was now gone.

Darnell and Leroy came on a Friday. This I remember because I had no homework to finish and was sitting alone in the room while Rosa and Bianca played tetherball outside with the other kids in the neighborhood. Shirley called to me from the kitchen.

"If you wanna see your brother, you better get ya butt out here! He ain't stayin all night."

I hurried to my feet, tripping over the comforter hanging from the edge of Bianca's bed and to the front room. I felt my legs grow heavy as I approached my destination. I never had recalled not wanted to see my brother so this emotion was completely foreign. I remained against the wall, my heart heavy with shame. I had not seen Darnell since before the incident and he knew me so well that I was sure he would be able to see right through me. I felt dirty all over again.

I could hear them conversing around the corner. Shirley as usual was all business and finances. Her words slurred which meant she had started her weekend early. She was complaining to Leroy that the payments were steadily decreasing and were not enough substantial enough to accommodate her for all the trouble I was causing. I sighed and caught a glimpse of my brother standing with his hands in his pockets and his head down. He looked older and depleted.

I wanted to run to him, to embrace him, to tell him that we should just run away all over again. Where didn't matter I just needed to be any place but here. The lump in my throat grew to ridiculous proportions and the tears began to fall. I tried to stifle my sobs to no avail.

"Bessie, what you doin' girl? Get out here and say Hi to Johnny. You act like he a stranger or somethin!" Shirley barked from the worn and dingy sofa, fingering the crisp bills.

Darnell looked up at me and immediately could tell something was wrong. Not only by the waterworks on display but also the fact that his little sister seemed to be withering away. I couldn't stop crying nor could I look him in the eye. I walked up to him and wrapped my arms around his waist, holding on tightly with my head buried deep in his chest.

He reached for my face and tried to turn my chin upward to him but I shook my head, turning away and began to wail louder.

"What did you do to her?" he asked, his voice threatening to a shout.

"I don't know what's wrong with that girl, ask her, not me!" Shirley was on the defense.

68

"What happened?" he had managed to pry my face to meet his eyes but I continued to shake my head and remain silent. I couldn't lie to him yet couldn't tell him the truth.

"Look, my man, whatever's up wit your sis, you gonna have to deal wit it later. You know we gotta be down at Sonny's by eight. I told you we wasn't stayin!"

I hadn't even noticed Leroy until then. I hated him. I hated all of them. Darnell shot him a piercing look out of the corner of his eye and leaned down to kiss me on my forehead. He pulled me closer to him, his fingers catching in my untidy curls.

"I'm coming back for you." He whispered.

My face was wet with a mixture of snot and tears and I couldn't move. I let him slide out of my embrace, my arms left limp at my side from his absence. I watched them leave and the stream of sorrow continued to pour out of me. Shirley remained seated on the couch, staring at me intently. She folded the stack of bills and tucked them neatly in her bra strap. I saw her mouth moving but everything was a fog, my ears were filled with a ringing sound as if someone had slapped me.

"What, are you deaf and dumb now?" she clapped her hands together loudly, snapping me back to reality "Go tell the girls to come here and you go to bed. Actin' like a fool, making people think somethin' wrong with you" she muttered under her breath.

I did as instructed, sending the girls out to the living room at their mother's request. I grabbed my cover and lay down on the floor, still dressed in my school clothes. I didn't care if I got in trouble or not. It was still early and I couldn't sleep, the shadows that lined the wall seemed to mock me. Silhouettes of trees branches swaying in the wind appeared to be pointing their bony fingers and shaking with laughter.

Sleep came sporadically. I awoke sweating profusely, the comforter tangled around my limbs constricting any movement. I tried to thrash unseen demons than were attempting to drown me in my own subconscious memory. I couldn't put it behind me. Time had done nothing to blur the incident from my mind. It was still fresh as blood and burned like the licking of blue flames.

The sun peeked through the curtains in a haze. I could tell by the chill in the air and the deafening silence that it was still too early to rise. I was tired, emotionally drained and my body felt stiff and sore. I was thoroughly exhausted despite what should have been at least ten hours of rest. My clothes were soaking wet from the intensity of dreams that tormented me through the night. I sat up and stared at the door, waiting for what I did not know. It was Saturday.

I quickly dressed and left the room, shutting the door behind me as not to wake the sleeping dragons. Apparently I had slept enough in order to gather my senses and change before Shirley awoke to find me in yesterday's clothes. The clock on the living room wall read 5:59am. I walked the length of the hall to the bathroom. After relieving myself I took a seat on the couch staring at the blank screen of the TV. I dared not touch the knobs or to make myself breakfast without permission. I had learned that almost any action on my part would most likely create a negative reaction from Shirley.

I heard the toilet flush and Bianca entered the room casting me a sideways glance. She stumbled toward the television in pink padded bunny slippers, their ears lopping from side to side, swaying with each step in cadence with her ponytail. She turned the knob until it clicked, then after an electrical popping and humming, Saturday morning cartoons filled the room, their joyous noise in direct opposition of my emotions.

She walked to the kitchen, returned with a bowl of Fruit Loops and took up position on the floor in front of the TV set, her back resting against the couch. I stared at her in disgust, watching the milk dribble down her chin as she consumed one bite after another, her mouth left open as she chewed. My mother would have never allowed for such a lack of manners. I would have traded anything in the world for the Buick with its cold cracked leather seats and faded interior.

The door of Shirley's bedroom creaked open and I could hear her shuffling down the hall. She stopped to peer into the girl's room then proceeded to use the bathroom. Bianca finished the remains of her breakfast and handed me the bowl.

"Here, put that in the kitchen"

I took it from her hands, rose from my seat on autopilot and went to set it in the already full sink. When I came back, Shirley had taken my place on the couch and was smoking a cigarette, inhaling the fumes through her nose and blowing a thick cloud of smoke from her mouth. She stared at me; eyes narrow as she flicked the ashes into the strategically placed ashtray resting on the arm of the couch. Her hatred for me was etched into her face like crow's feet. It was 7:32am.

There were no sirens, only the flashing of red and blue lights as the squad car rolled to a stop in front of the house. I had never seen the woman move so fast. Shirley extinguished her cigarette and ran to the back room, almost tripping over her feet in haste.

"You little bitch!" she muttered. I was used to being blamed for everything but I was completely oblivious to what she thought I had done now.

I could make out the sound of her rummaging through drawers, slamming them with force but couldn't take my eyes off the window. Through the separation in the thin curtains I watched as two officers in dark blue uniforms approached, coming up the walkway. One of them held a clipboard in hand and the other was talking into some kind of radio or walkie talkie positioned on his shoulder. I could see their guns holstered at their side in thick leather belts encircling their waists.

Bianca froze, her eyes growing wide and she started to cry. With a father like mine I had been raised to be weary of law enforcement. "The heat, the fuzz, the man" were phrases used in my household to describe them and more often than not, they came with trouble. I, at this time, was more curios than frightened. I couldn't imagine a fate worse than my present situation so I had no concerns about the outcome. A part of me had always assumed Shirley and her associates were involved in illegal activities to some extent and I had known from the beginning that Leroy was up to no good.

The doorbell rang and I can't deny a part of me delighted in seeing Bianca in such a state. She cried out for her mother, fear spanning her face as she looked about wildly with no idea what to do. Shirley approached from down the hall. She had managed to pull herself somewhat together, ironically dressed in the purple muumuu she had worn the first day I met her. Yesterday's mascara was still smeared around circumference of her eyes and her wig had shifted somewhat to the side, making her face appear to be off center. She fidgeted nervously, shifting her glance around the house which was in disarray.

The knock that commenced was forceful and full of authority. One of the policemen approached the living room window and peered in, meeting my eyes. He stepped back and I could see his lips moving as he leaned in toward his partner to speak.

The second knock was accompanied by a command.

"LAPD, open the door."

Shirley gave me an evil glare as she walked past me.

"You better keep your mouth shut" she hissed.

I had no idea what she expected me to say anyways. Bianca hadn't moved from her location, she was chewing at her fingers and making whimpering sounds. Shirley stepped over her on the way to the front door instructing her to get up and sit on the couch. She obliged, taking a seat next to me. Apparently given the situation she didn't have a problem with being that close. Her fear of what was going to happen was far greater than her dislike for me. I swear she even scooted closer.

Shirley straightened her wig before grabbing the knob with a trembling hand. She opened the door just a crack at first.

"Can I help you?"

I had never heard her be so polite and quite honestly I didn't think it was possible. She flashed a smile and stepped aside allowing the two men to enter.

"Are you Shirley Gonzalez?" the taller of the men asked as he stepped over the threshold.

He wasn't looking at her when he spoke; his dark eyes were trained directly on me with suspicion. This was the point in time I began to feel uneasy. The other officer with sandy brown hair and glasses walked past them both to the hall, then turned on his heels to survey the kitchen. He plucked a pen from behind his ear and began to make notes on the clipboard.

"Yes, I am. What's going on?" her voice was beginning to waver.

"Is this your daughter?" he pointed to Bianca. Apparently he was letting it be known he was the one asking the questions as he offered no response to hers.

"Yes"

"Who is this girl?" pointing to me.

She hesitated. I could tell the wheels in her head were turning as she was trying to predict where this line of questioning was headed. She had a decision to make.

"Maam, what is this girl's relation to you?" his voice was firm and resonated with bass matching his height and muscular build. He was definitely a no nonsense guy and would not tolerate her stalling.

"She's, uh, a friend of the family."

In a sentence, I was disowned from being her niece and honestly had no hard feelings. I shifted nervously on the couch. I knew now their visit was on my behalf and I couldn't fathom for the life of me what I had done. I thought maybe one the girls had done something bad at school and blamed it on me. I didn't like living with Shirley's one bit but with weighing jail in the other hand I would almost rather stick it out. Bianca turned me with her mouth ajar, her tears had subsided. She must have been thinking the same thing.

The other officer approached me and stooped down until his eyes were level with mine. I could see my frightened reflection in his glasses.

"Anna, don't worry. We're going to get you out of here and back to your parents. Your brother is waiting in the car."

It was strange hearing my name again. My heart went from sinking in my chest to jumping with joy. I didn't understand what was happening or how they found out about us but that didn't matter. I began to laugh and cry simultaneously. He took me by the hand, helping me rise to my feet and guided me out the front door. I looked back over my shoulder at Shirley. Her mouth was hanging wide open and she looked confused, almost betrayed.

I traveled down the concrete walkway for what would be the last time, past the dying grass and the yellow ball that dangled there, suspended on its leash. A prisoner, just like I had been for the last few months. I never again played tetherball again. It would always remind me of this place.

Darnell's face was pressed again the glass anxiously awaiting my arrival. Officer Collins, whom had disclosed his name to me on our short journey to the car, opened the back door and I slid onto the leather seat right into my brothers open arms. He was crying and I could feel his bony frame trembling as he held me.

"I'm sorry, sis. I'm so sorry!" his voice was jagged, hoarse.

He buried his face in the crook of my neck. I tried to relay to him that he didn't have anything to be sorry for, that none one of it was his fault. He didn't hear me and I don't think he wanted to. He needed someone to blame and he was placing the burden on his own thin shoulders. He had changed so much in the last four months. I could see it in his face yesterday. The strange thing was that all of our childhood we thought ourselves miserable based on our circumstances but until recently I had never seen him so despondent.

When I think back to before we left, I remember him smiling, the wide grin of my father and my mother's laughter. True, our upbringing was unconventional to say the least and we endured more than our fair share of beatings but there was also beauty. My mother loved us fiercely and though I never once heard my father utter the words, I know he did as well. For the first time, I thought about how my parents must feel. Their only two children were gone, had disappeared mid day from a public park and never returned. They must have thought we had been kidnapped or possibly even killed. Nothing they had ever done had made them worthy of enduring such anguish.

Officer Collins sat in the front seat of the squad car talking on the CB radio. He kept his voice at a minimal tone so I couldn't make out the conversation only bits and pieces were audible. I could make out something about "children's home" and "investigation" but nothing more.

"Are they taking us back to Mom and Dad now?" I asked.

All I wanted to do was to see my parents, apologize and hug them for at least an hour. I knew they would be furious that we had run away and was scared beyond measure of what my father would do to us when we returned but I didn't care anymore.

"I don't know"

"Officer Collins, can we see our parents now?" I asked timidly.

"Well, there's a process we have to follow. Your brother told me about what was going on at home and we have to make sure things are going to be okay. Officer Whitman and I are going to take you somewhere where you will be safe."

Another patrol car pulled up behind us and two more officers exited the vehicle, one of them a woman. Officer Collins got out of our car and joined them on the sidewalk for what I suppose was a debriefing. He motioned toward us and then pointed up at the house. They approached the front door in unison. I could see Shirley just beyond the entryway. She was waving her arms about hysterically and looked like she was crying.

We were left alone in the car for a good half hour and neither of us said much. We were both wondering about this "process" there was to follow and where we would go from here. At least we were together. Officers Collins and Whitman returned and assured us everything would be fine. They radioed in to someone saying they were on the way and we sped off, no need now for flashing lights or sirens.

The drive was long as we traveled through parts of Los Angeles we had never seen before. These were the nicer homes with manicured yards and tall palm trees lining the streets. I felt more and more relieved with each passing mile taking me farther away from Shirley's home and the ordeal I had recently been through. I would never have to see Juan again and for the first time in a long time, I smiled.

III.

The car slowed in front of a large white building with several small cottages surrounding it along with a large fence that spanned the perimeter of the property. The words on the sign we passed by on approach read "Los Angeles County Juvenile Hall". After parking in a space near the entrance, Officer Whitman gathered his paperwork together neatly and got out, opening the back door on Darnell's side.

"C'mon son, we're here." He held out his hand as to guide him from the car and I scooted over following suit. "No sugar, just him. You can't stay here, you're not old enough."

I was confused and so was Darnell. We looked at each other in disbelief. We had been separated for months this wasn't supposed to be happening. I began to cry, my chest felt tight and my stomach was in knots. Darnell sat back down next to me.

"I can't leave her again!" he shouted at him.

"Look son, we'll make sure she's taken care of. We'll get you both back to your parents soon enough."

"I don't care, you don't understand, she trusted me and I left her. Something bad happened to her and it's my fault. I can't leave her again!" he was on the verge of tears once more.

"No, Darnell, don't leave me" I screamed and starting kicking at the seat, pleading with the officers. "Don't take him away, please! Please don't take him!"

"I'll get her calmed down. Go on, they're waiting for him" Officer Collins volunteered from the driver's seat.

Whitman grabbed Darnell by the arm and led him away from the car. I could see Darnell jerking his arm away and Whitman leaned into him, whispering something in her ear and he immediately calmed down. He looked over his shoulder, tears in his eyes and mouthed "I'm sorry".

I screamed bloody murder. Collins got out of the front seat, walked around the vehicle and came to sit down beside me. I moved as far away from him as possible, my head pressed against the opposite window, body flush with the hard interior of the door. I would have gotten out and run after them but the back of the squad car wasn't equipped with any door handles.

"Honey, try to calm down. This isn't forever, you'll see him soon." He reached into his pocket and pulled out a piece of bubble gum. "Here, for you"

I didn't want gum, I wanted my brother. He explained this was where Darnell had to stay while they contacted my parents and only until then. He told me I was going to stay with a nice lady who takes care of children that were in the same situation as I was. He reached into his other pocket and pulled out a notebook scribbled a phone number on it, tore out its page and handed it to me.

"This is the number to where your brother is, you may not be able to talk to him right away if you call but you will always know where he is at. Officer Whitman is going to do the same for Darnell. It will be alright, Anna, trust me, okay?"

I didn't trust him but I took the paper anyways. I looked at the writing scrawled over it and it made me feel a little better, only slightly. He held out the piece of gum again which I accepted this time but only to hold captive in my fist. I stared past him out the window and searched for any sign of my brother or his partner but they were no longer in sight. They had entered the building and were long gone. I continued to cry like a baby, snot dripping from my nose. He handed me a Kleenex then pulled his wallet out of his pocket and began to show me pictures of his family. He had a daughter about my age and in the photos she was smiling and holding a baby.

"These are my kids. My daughter is five just like you and she's learning to play the piano. She loves music. What do you like to do?"

He was doing a terrible job of trying to distract me. I sobbed louder while he continued to talk about his children and their extracurricular activities which at the time I cared absolutely nothing about. It had only been about fifteen minutes but it seemed like an hour before Officer Whitman returned to the car. Collins again took his position behind the wheel and I must have fallen asleep on the drive. When I awoke we were traveling into what appeared to be the mountains, the road twisting and turning with trees lining the hillside.

We arrived at a home with a Spanish tile roof and a large fully functional fountain in the front yard. Flowers of every color decorated the landscape and it was the most beautiful home I had ever seen. It was however viewed through blurred vision. I had awakened crying and the chance of my tears subsiding anytime soon was minimal. Both officers walked me up the steps to a set of double doors meant for a giant. When the remarkably large doors swung open, we were met by an older lady with a thin frame, red hair and a perfect smile.

She introduced herself as Maggie and gave me a tour of her home. Collins and Whitman followed at our heels, in awe as well at the splendor of the house. She showed me to a small room adorned in shades of pink and purple where everything matched down to the small throw rugs and decorative bed pillows and informed me this was where I would sleep. I had never seen anything like it. I wished for an instant that I could stop crying, tell her how beautiful it was but I was miserable and unless she were to pull Darnell out of one of the many walk-in closets, that wasn't going to change.

She offered the two policemen coffee which they declined saying they had to be on their way. Officer Collins gave me a hug and reminded me about the slip of paper he had given me, telling me to keep it safe and that my brother was only a phone call away. Maggie escorted me to the living room, turned on the television and brought me a plate of cookies and a glass of milk on a fold up tray, willing me to make myself at home.

I dozed off on the plush lavender couch, slumped to one side and my face stained with tears. She woke me and handed me a set of freshly washed, folded pajamas covered with teddy bears wearing little pink tutus.

"I'll run you a bath after dinner and you can sleep in these. You can go set them on your bed for now."

She went on to explain that she couldn't have any children of her own but would often have other children come to live with her while their parents were going through a "transitional period". Right now, I was the only one here and therefore she would be spoiling me rotten so I would just have to get used to it. She was the nicest woman I had ever met.

"Come and eat, sweetheart" she called from the kitchen, her voice was melodic.

She had set a perfect table for two and there were fresh cut white roses along with other flowers from her garden that I couldn't name in shades of yellow and orange as the centerpiece. We ate in silence even though I wanted to talk to her. I felt as though I should but I couldn't bring myself open my mouth aside from filling it with the homemade lasagna she had pulled recently out of the oven.

"Thank you, Miss Maggie" I managed to mumble as she was clearing the table of dishes.

"You're welcome, Anna" she smiled. "You're a very polite little girl aren't you? Your parents must have raised you well."

I wish she wouldn't have brought up the subject, my lip began to quiver and my eyes lowered to my bare feet.

"Oh, I'm sorry sweetie. I didn't mean to…" her voice trailed off and she looked away.

"It's okay." I quickly said, blinking repeatedly to prevent the tears from falling "Can I get ready for bed now?"

She nodded, walked down the long hallway to the bathroom and began to run the water for my bath. I followed and stood in the doorway watching her. I reached in my pocket for the paper with Darnell's phone number so it wouldn't be lost and came across the piece of gum Collins had given me in the squad car. I removed it from its wrapper and popped the purple cube in my mouth, chewing slowly. I had never had bubble gum before, only the minty kind that came in sticks. This was grape flavored and tasted like pure sugar. It was delicious.

After my bath I dressed in the pajamas Maggie had given me that, like magic, ended up being exactly my size. The room was equipped with a night light and she left the door cracked open "just in case I needed anything". I got under the covers and turned over trying to sleep but it evaded me. I missed Darnell and my parents more than ever. I began to sob loudly, covering my mouth with the pillow so Maggie wouldn't hear. Eventually my eyelids became heavy and I cried myself to sleep.

Even though my daytime situation appeared to have greatly improved, my nightmares bore the same anguish and intensity. Juan paraded around in my dreams like a madman, which wasn't far from reality. I tossed and turned throughout the night waking intermittently to find myself alone, drenched in sweat and tears. The last few months played over and over in my mind like a malfunctioning phonograph.

The next morning I arose on my own accord and thought I was still dreaming. It took several minutes before I placed my surroundings and refreshed my memory of the prior day's occurrences. I sat up on the edge of the bed and found little pink slippers on the floor right where I had positioned my feet. Things were just too perfect here and the thought of pinching myself actually crossed my mind.

I raised my hand to scratch my head and that's when I felt it. My hair was matted and stuck together in a huge glob. I moved my fingers over the clump, it was soft and sticky. I smelled my hand... grape. I was crying so hard last night and so upset I had forgotten to get rid of the bubble gum I was chewing and during the night it had not only gotten in my hair but was also stuck on the pillow where I laid my head. The last thing I wanted to do was make Maggie angry with me and on my first night here, I had ruined her linen and not to mention, my own hair.

The aroma of bacon filled my nostrils and I could faintly hear music playing. I needed to use the bathroom and had to figure a way to get the gum out of my hair before she saw me. No such luck, Maggie appeared in the doorway drying her hands on a kitchen towel. Her smile turned to not anger, but concern.

"Oh my goodness, Anna, what happened to your hair?" she exclaimed.

"I fell asleep with gum in my mouth and I ruined your pillowcase, I'm so sorry Miss Maggie" my voice was barely audible and my gaze downcast, studying the circular purple rug interwoven with fine pink strands in an intricate butterfly design.

"I don't care about the pillowcase, honey. We have to get that out of your hair!"

She reached her delicate fingers to my head and began attempting to separate the tangled mess to no avail, biting her lip in frustration.

"Oh, my bacon!" she hurried out of the room and called to me from down the hall, headed for the kitchen "Be right back!"

I slipped my feet into the house shoes she had set out for me and padded down the hall to the bathroom. The walls were lined with framed paintings of flowers in shades of various pastel colors. I recognized that most of them were lilies with the occasional tulip breaking the monotony. The bathroom was ornamented in every hue of green imaginable with dark brown accents. It was like walking into a forest.

I relieved myself and washed my face, wiping the counter down after me. Everything in the house was spotless and I didn't want to be the one to leave it otherwise. The porcelain sparkled and shone reflecting off the crystal light fixtures displaying an array of rainbow colors around the room that was almost enchanting. I wondered what Darnell was doing. From what I gathered on my brief visit in front of the Juvenile Hall, they didn't possess even half of the comforts and amenities as my current residence. I wondered what time they served breakfast.

Maggie knocked softly at the door. I opened it and she entered with extra towels and a jar of peanut butter. The confusion must have been written all over my face. She laughed gently as she removed the lid set it on the counter then proceeded to wrap one of the towels around my neck and shoulders.

"Well, I must say, in all my years of caring for children, I haven't had to deal with this situation. However I did read somewhere that the oils in peanut butter are good for getting gum out hair. I know it sounds crazy but I'm up for giving it a try. What do you say?"

At that moment, any worries or apprehension I had retained dissipated in the curves of her smile and I nodded my head in agreement. She scooped out a glob of the thick, creamy substance with a tablespoon, smearing it onto her hands and then into my hair. She rubbed it in and tried to comb through it with her fingers as well as she could but it didn't seem to be working.

After a good fifteen minutes she had only managed to remove a small portion of the gum but had succeeded in covering my head with almost the entire jar of peanut butter. She instructed me to place my head in the sink and retrieved a bottle of shampoo and conditioner from the shower. It took three washings to rid my hair of the peanut butter and I was left with a soaking wet clump still entwined with a light shade of purple.

Maggie shook her head in dismay, left the room and came back momentarily with a pair of large scissors. My eyes grew wide and my mouth dropped open, I didn't want her to cut my hair off! I had been mistaken for a boy enough times in my life already and this would do nothing but seal the deal.

"I'm sorry, sweetheart, but I'm out of options here."

She approached and I retreated, backing myself into the corner between the vanity and the commode. She looked helpless. I could tell by her pained expression that this act would bring her no joy. She paused, letting the hand holding the scissors drop to her side and sat down on the toilet seat beside me, patting the tops of her thighs lightly, motioning me to sit on her lap. I obliged, on the verge of tears.

"This isn't turning out to be a very good start to the morning for us, is it?" she placed the scissors on the counter, picked up a towel and continued to pat my hair dry.

I shook my head, no. She promised not to cut much of my hair, only around the matted area and then try to comb the rest out. She said I could watch her the whole entire time and that she would stop if I asked her to. I agreed and the process went rather smoothly with me studying each and every snip in the mirror, wincing as I saw my hair fall onto the tile floor. It was the first time I had ever had a haircut and honestly when she was done, you couldn't really tell the difference in length. All the split ends were gone and it was fairly even.

By the time we seated ourselves at the dining table, breakfast was cold. The scrambled eggs had started to harden around the edges and she said I didn't have to eat them. This I was glad for as I couldn't stand eggs anyway, no matter how they were cooked. We both settled on cold cereal but didn't let the bacon go to waste.

After the meal, we cleaned the breakfast dishes together, she washed and I dried. When we were done, Maggie showed me the other rooms in the house. She explained it was a five bedroom that she had lived in it alone since her husband had passed away more than seven years ago. It was then that she decided to open up her home to less fortunate children. She enjoyed their company and the different personalities of all the boys and girls that passed through her custom made French doors.

She had a den that was filled from ceiling to floor with books, just like a library. There was a section for children that housed all of the classics as well as many picture books written by modern authors that boasted silly titles. I crooked my head to the side, surveying them one by one and finally rested my hand upon the spine of The Swiss Family Robinson, earning a smile from Maggie.

"Can you read that?" she questioned, eyebrows raised.

"Yes, my mom taught me to read a long time ago. We never had a TV." I replied, as if that single statement would explain everything. Perhaps it did, she nodded with understanding, obviously impressed.

"Keep that with you, at least I know you will put it to use."

We exited the room and she shut the door gently behind us. We continued down the hall, opening each door as we went. The next room was decorated in shades of blue and housed a set of bunk beds, two dressers and a large chest positioned in the far corner. The walls were decorated with assorted sports memorabilia and throw rugs the shape and design of baseball diamonds adorned the floor.

Maggie explained she wanted to have a place for boys and girls to feel equally at home. We were all princes and princesses in our own right, she said and since whenever children came to her they were most likely saddened by having to be away from their parents in the first place so she wanted to provide them with the very best.

The next room was similar to mine with only a single twin bed but it was painted a light hue of yellow with pink and green accents.

Instead of butterflies, there were flowers displayed on the rugs and comforter. It looked like a secret garden. I smiled. Any child lucky enough to find a home with Maggie, even temporarily, would indeed be subject to spurts of happiness. There was no way around it.

"You're really nice, Miss Maggie." I looked up at her, still smiling.

"You don't have to call me Miss Maggie, sweetheart. Maggie will do, and thank you." She gave my shoulders a quick squeeze in appreciation for my sentiments.

The other rooms of her home were equally as beautiful. I had seen most of them yesterday when she gave me the condensed tour accompanied by Officers Collins and Whitman. What she hadn't shown us then, was her backyard. It was tremendous and looked like a botanical garden. Orange and lemon trees lined the perimeter and on each side were wooden beds that were home to what seemed to be at least twenty different kinds of flowers.

I waited for Darnell to call but he never did. Of course, I ended up losing the piece of paper Collins gave me after all so Maggie help me find the number to the Juvenile Hall in the phone book. I finally tried to reach Darnell on my third day there and was instructed by someone who answered the phone to leave my number and that he would be returning my call shortly. It was four hours before he called back.

"Darnell" I asked when Maggie handed me the receiver.

"Yeah, sis, it's me" he responded wearily "Are you okay?"

"I'm fine, the lady I'm staying with is really nice Darnell. Do you like it there?"

"No."

"Are they being mean to you?"

"Look Anna, I really don't wanna talk about it. I just wanna get out of here." I could tell in his voice he was fighting back tears."

"Did they tell you when we get to see Mom and Dad?"

"No, all they said was that they found them and since we were in the court system now, they would have to go through them to get us back."

I didn't know what that meant but it didn't sound good. I was worried about my brother, he sounded so worn out, not like himself but we had both changed dramatically over the last few months and it was definitely taking its toll.

"I miss you, Darnell, and I miss Mom!"

"I know, I know... me too."

"Maggie is really nice and I have a room all to myself, she took me shopping and bought me some clothes yesterday." I was trying to cheer him up but not thinking about my selfishness when he was obviously miserable.

"That's great, sis" he tried to sound happy but his efforts were in vain "I have to go now, I'll try to call you tomorrow but we can't have many phone calls here."

I could hear a commotion in the background, the sound of shouting and what seemed like chairs scraping against the floor. He hung up without saying goodbye and I was left holding the receiver until the dial tone blared in my ear. Maggie took the phone from my hand and placed it back in its cradle.

"Don't worry, honey, he will be alright." she smoothed back my hair "Let's get you some lunch"

The time I spent with Maggie was unforgettable. As much as she spoiled me, taking me shopping for the frilly dresses I always wanted and indulging me with endless books from her library to keep me occupied, I still longed everyday to go home to my parents and my brother. The problem was, I didn't know where home would be.

She taught me about gardening on which subject she was obviously an expert. She showed me how to turn over the soil and plant the seeds just far enough in the ground so they would stay in place yet be able to absorb the water and sunlight in order to grow. I had told her that I wanted to plant my own so she let me pick a spot in the yard for a peach tree. I placed the seed carefully and perfectly. For the next few weeks, tending to it was my sole purpose in life.

I watered it daily and then the results started showing. A tiny sprig of green peered up from beneath the dirt and I was overly excited. I continued to care for it but with patience not being my virtue, I decided to water it more and more frequently hoping it would grow even faster. It was on a Saturday morning when I walked into the backyard with the ruler she had given me to measure its progress only to find the small stem laying on its side withering away.

I ran back into the house slamming the door behind me, face wet tears. Maggie approached me and asked me what was wrong. I told her what had happened and she explained that I had given It too much water but assured me that we would try again later.

"You mean I drowned it?" I asked, sniffling.

"Well, that's a little harsh, it's just a plant but we will just be more careful next time."

She went on to explain that some things just take time and it isn't in our hands or our ability to change that. She related it to my current situation and the time I was spending with her.

"Life sometimes is a waiting game. There is no way around it. When you try to speed up the process, it will end up doing more harm than good. Patience is something we have to learn and trust me, it's to our benefit. We can't rush things and we can't play God. There is a plan for us all, even little peaches, sweetheart."

I told her I didn't want to plant any more seeds. I had killed the first thing I had tried to grow and I felt terrible. The rest of the day I spent in my room by choice. I sat on my bed with the most recent book I had gotten from the shelves of her den and wrapped myself in the pages of Heidi for the next three days.

It had been a little over a month before Maggie got the call that my presence was requested down at the courthouse. My parents would be there and we were scheduled for a visit. I didn't understand why I just couldn't go home with them then. She went on to explain that there would be other people in attendance, police officers and counselors that wanted to see how we interacted and would most likely be asking us all a lot of questions.

I had been through something similar once before. Almost two years earlier, our family had been staying in a motel in San Diego and my brother and I had been left alone in the room for three days while our parents "tied up some loose ends" in Mexico. On the third day, the maid had alerted the manager who, in turn, called the police. The officers then had taken us both to a Children's home where we stayed two days until my parents returned.

I was younger then so I don't remember much but I do recall them asking my brother and I questions about how we were treated, whether our parents beat us, if we were eating, going to school and things like that. Then they sat us all down around a big table in a little room and asked us the same questions over and over again. I remember lying.

Maggie laid my clothes out neatly on the bed the morning of the scheduled appointment. She had selected me to wear a teal satin dress with a big collar and white bobby socks. The patent leather Mary Janes she had purchased were neatly placed on the floor on top of the butterfly rug. I dressed and sat down at the dining table but couldn't eat a thing. My stomach was in knots. It had been over five months since I had seen my parents.

The drive to the courthouse was long and unnerving. I played out the scenario repeatedly in my mind. I had no idea what I would say when I saw them. I knew I couldn't wait to hug my mother yet I was terrified to face my father. Maggie had said they would bring Darnell as well and for that little bit of relief, I was thrilled.

When we arrived in front of the large white building she found a parking spot in the lot that was almost already filled to capacity. As we exited the car, my knees grew wobbly. She came around to meet me and we walked hand in hand into the courthouse. She looked at the paperwork she carried with her in a large manila envelope for the correct room number and realized our location was on the second floor.

There were benches positioned in the hall for those who were either waiting their turn or for visitors awaiting the outcome of trials. My mother was seated on a one of the wooden benches twisting her hands in her lap nervously and my father paced back and forth in front of her. I stopped in my tracks.

"Is that them?" Maggie leaned down to whisper in my ear.

I nodded my head in agreement but didn't budge. There were still about thirty feet between us and they hadn't yet seen me. Honestly they probably wouldn't recognize me holding the hand of this older white woman, decked out in frills and lace. My heartbeat increased and my head swooned. My father had his back to us and I watched slowly as my mother rose to her feet and burst into tears.

I broke free of Maggie's grip and ran to her. She lifted me in her arms and twirled me around, sobbing uncontrollably. I met my father's gaze while still wrapped in her embrace. He was smiling at me. I smiled back as my mother placed me back on solid ground. I then stepped slowly into the strong arms of my father.

"Hey kid." His deep voice has lost some of its power and force.

"Hi, Daddy, I'm sorry" the words choked in my throat and came out harsh and guttural.

"You don't worry about that, you're here now and that's all that matters."

I sat down between the two of them as they simultaneously wrapped their arms around my shoulders. Maggie approached and introduced herself, shaking hands with both of my parents. Seating herself on the bench on the opposite side, she fiddled in her purse and leafed through paperwork. I could tell she was nervous.

Darnell arrived within the next five minutes escorted by a police officer. He kept his eyes cast downward and refused to look at my father. He hugged them both but lacked sincerity in his side of the embrace. I know he was worried about the outcome and dealing with the brunt of my father's wrath. My mother scooted over to make room for him on the bench and we remained there, scrunched together like a can of sardines until they called our names.

I automatically assumed we would be in an actual courtroom with a judge who donned a black robe and carried a gavel like I had seen in old Perry Mason reruns. Our small meeting would take place in one of the much smaller adjacent rooms. The series of questioning left my mother in tears. There was a stenographer present who typed away at a little machine recording the entire conversation.

They asked us questions about why we had run away, asked my mother and father about their current situation and whether they believed themselves fit to take care of children. The anger on my father's face was apparent but he maintained his composure, answering questions with "Yes sir" and "No sir".

I learned during the inquisition that my parents had obtained a stable residence as they were asked to provide proof. My mother slid a lease agreement across the table along with letters of character and reference. I remained as quiet and still as possible only speaking when spoken to, on my best behavior. Darnell looked bored and fidgeted with his fingers. I could feel the vibrations and hear the slight tapping of his foot banging against the metal leg of the table.

As the interview drew to a close, we said our goodbyes tearfully and parted ways. When we reached the car I was still crying and Maggie tried to console me. She said she had been in this situation before and it wouldn't be long before we were reunited permanently and not to worry, that the interview had gone better than planned. She suggested ice cream.

It was a week later before we were notified that we could go home. Darnell had called me excited, saying that on Thursday he would be released and we would all be scheduled for another meeting at the same location. Maggie helped me pack. She allowed me take along all of the clothes she had purchased for me and let me pick three of my favorite books to keep as my own, one being, of course, The Swiss Family Robinson.

I told her I would miss her as I climbed in the back seat of her green Volvo for the last time. She said I was welcome to come back to visit and told me that I would always be one of her favorites. The long journey this time found me happy. Smiling, I looked out the window at the sun sparkling through the treetops as we descended down the hills and around the curves.

The courthouse was just as crowded as before and the room our meeting was to take place in today was two doors down from last time. Darnell was already standing there with my parents when Maggie and I arrived. I looked at them as I approached, my family, imperfect but mine. We embraced... all of us together, smiling. My mother shook Maggie's hand and thanked her for taking such good care of her daughter and my father nodded in agreement. Once my parents completed stack after stack of paperwork, we were free to go.

The blue Buick was parked in the lot and still remained the same. I remember the day we decided to leave, the way the milk dripped down its glass window, like clouded tears. My father put his arm around my shoulder guiding me in the back seat, its faded leather cracked and now hot to the touch. My brother scooted in beside me as my mother climbed in front and my father finally took his place behind the wheel. Their doors closed in unison.

On the way to our new home, my father apologized to my brother and I, promising to never lay a hand on us again. My mother expressed her worry, saying that she thought we both had been killed. I looked into her face and saw that she had aged. There were touches of gray sprouting from her hairline and her face seemed more wrinkled and her posture more slouched.

The residence ended up being a beautiful six bedroom home in the Santa Barbara hills without a lick of furniture. My father had talked the owner into letting us live there rent free for two months while my parents got back on their feet as he had taken pity on our predicament. The two months ended up being four and the fifth month found us living in garage as the owner had evicted us and taken back the keys. With the home now being up for sale, we were forced to hide, keeping quiet so he wouldn't know we were there when he would arrive intermittently with perspective buyers.

We were discovered within a few weeks and when threatened with the police, returned our belongings and ourselves back to the Buick. Three daily meals ended up being a conversation between my brother and I that started always started with "remember when" and the promise my father made to us was only half kept. He never laid another finger on Darnell after our return but I was a different story. His good intentions lasted only three months before my tan skin was spotted with shades of black and blue.

My childhood was never pretty. My parents definitely had their share of shortcomings yet I realize now it has built my character and my strength. God places people in our lives for a reason, even our parents. We don't get to decide what family we will be born into, who we will call our mother and father. I know now that nothing I experienced in my upbringing was so called normal but I also took notice that during the months in my parents' absence, I never smiled, I never laughed and I never loved.

I wish I could say that things got better when we returned from LA, but I can't. I did realize that my mother and father loved me and though they might not have known how to always show it and may not have made the right decisions, we always remained a family. Some people don't have that option. Regardless of circumstances, the grass isn't always greener on the other side, sometimes it's only Astroturf, an artificial façade.

I finally get it. There are some choices we are allowed to make and sometimes the outcomes of our lives are left solely in the hands of fate. I thought I would die in Los Angeles… honestly a part of me did. It changed me. It changed both of us but we endured and we survived.

Anna Marie

Of All the Chances

By

Caroline Swanson

If I am being honest,
We probably would not have worked out anyway

But I wish we'd had the chance to break up
Because we quarreled over the ethics
Of how to deal with a baby rabbit who broke its back at the bottom of a cage
Or
The chance to break up because I forgot to close
The child's gate and your dog shredded the comforter
You've had since you were twelve
Or
The chance to break up because the distance was
The reason you didn't want to be close to me
Or
The chance to break up for some other fundamental reason
Other than because someone showed you the profanist way of "making love"

The Chance to trust yourself enough to be loved or touched
Without an abuse of trust I didn't commit
The Chance to use my hands where you were violently raped
In the hope of serving justice in this most sacred way
And more than that,
The Chance to look at and touch
The parts of me that were meant for you to explore

The Chance to touch you in the way that teaches you how to trust again
The Chance that opens the gateway
To the fear you bottled up inside skin and blood and bones

The chance that makes you coffee in the morning
And takes your dog for walks while you're still asleep
From a night filled with insomniac dreams and grinding teeth

The chance that wears her sexiest underwear
And travels thousands of miles to meet you more than halfway

The chance to finally be in the same place
For an extended time

Tablespoons of Tears

The chance that gets to hear how lucky you are to have me
And the chance to prove it everyday

The chance to say, YES, I will, Yes, I do

The chance that births new life
And raises it as the love which grows between us each day

The chance that assigns our parting only to death

All of this is to say
I miss the chances
As they might have happened

When All Hope Is Gone, God Is Still There
By
Linda LeMaire

That which does not kill us makes us stronger.

Friedrich Nietzsche

My story is about the amazing miracles I experienced after deadly spinal meningitis and encephalitis mysteriously invaded my body after an emergency spine surgery—almost stealing my very life and destroying my brain. It is about God's awesome power triumphing over medical facts when my physicians stated there was no hope for healing me, and wanted to unplug my ventilator… ending my life quickly. *Above all, it's a story of hope, restoration, and answered prayer in the face of impossible obstacles on my journey "through the valley of the shadow of death."*

Out of the blue, in a single, ordinary day, life changed radically for me when sudden horrific back pain led to emergency spine surgery. That surgery became the gateway by which viral herpes simplex spinal meningitis entered my body. There was a 1 in 500,000 chance of getting this rare disease. I then contracted the most dreadful side effect—deadly encephalitis. The horrific pain, mental delusion, respiratory failure, speech failure, coma, seizures and paralysis all left me lying flat on my back for almost nine weeks. I was mostly unconscious and totally unaware that I hovered weeks on end, between life and death.

Most of what happened to me was so shocking and—on the face of it—almost unbelievable, that it has taken diligence to put together the facts of the mind-boggling roller coaster of events I experienced. Since I was mostly unconscious during my hospital saga, I had to study my hospital medical records, have discussions with my doctors and nurses, with my husband as well as with family and friends to learn what actually happened. What I discovered is that my journey was a horrifying and excruciating nightmare that only God could bring me through.

Doctors told my husband the odds were overwhelming against my survival. However, they said, even if I lived, my chances of having *normal* brain function were zero. They urged my husband to authorize turning off my ventilator… to let me die quickly.

In spite of the grim medical prognoses and the disturbing facts of my condition, God upended the medical reality so dramatically that even my spine doctor marveled a few months later, "*You are a miracle!*"

I am completely in awe and deeply humbled at how dramatically God brought me through… the valley of the shadow of death.

But… I need to go back to where it all started…

****

Thursday July 11, 2013 began like any other day. My husband Dave and I took a walk, had breakfast, did chores, and ran errands. At about 7:00 PM, we went to Bible study at a neighbor's house. Nothing unusual had happened all day.

Then… at about 7:15 PM, while simply sitting on the sofa, I suddenly experienced waves of unbearable back pain that took my breath away. Terrified, I grabbed my husband and told him we had to go home immediately. There was no time to explain anything to anyone.

In the car, I'm sure I sounded like a mad woman, alternately telling Dave to take me home; then, *no*, take me to the hospital. We chose home—only about five minutes away—but by the time we got inside the house, I was screaming—and couldn't stop. The pain felt like it was pounding the life out of me.

In the car, I'm sure I sounded like a mad woman, alternately telling Dave to take me home; then, *no*, take me to the hospital. We chose home—only about five minutes away—but by the time we got inside the house, I was screaming—and couldn't stop. The pain felt like it was pounding the life out of me.

My husband was bewildered at my strange behavior, but while still trying to make sense of things, he managed to call 911. The paramedics arrived in minutes with lights flashing and sirens blaring.

They seemed to take forever as they conducted their evaluation. Eventually they concluded that I must be having a heart attack since my blood pressure was 227/125 and my left arm pain, along with my throbbing back, was agonizing. So they bundled me into an ambulance for a ride to the hospital, which is about 13 miles away, and where the best heart specialists in the region practice.

In my agony, it seemed like the ambulance was barely crawling along. (I felt like I could *walk* faster.) Adding to my distress, the paramedics refused to give me any medication at all for fear of obscuring the cause of the pain. I was so miserable that I actually told them that I wanted *out* of the ambulance since they weren't going to help me. They laughed and tightened the straps on the gurney even tighter.

At the hospital, after several tests including a CT scan and an MRI, the medical staff concluded that I was *not* having a heart attack. Even though they still didn't know what *was* going on, they gave me Morphine and I began to feel some relief.

I hardly noticed when I was bundled into *Ambulance #2* for the lengthy ride to *the next hospital in* Roseville, about 20 miles away. As it turned out, this ambulance ride was only the second of *three* rides I would have to *three* different hospitals before a treatment plan would finally be carried out the next day.

At Hospital #2, a spinal tap and ultrasound showed a large mysterious mass on my spine in the upper thoracic region. The doctors speculated that it was possibly from an infection—which made no sense—or something else caused by trauma—which hadn't happened to me. The mass was pressing on nerves in my spine— causing horrendous pain and threatening my life. They concluded that I needed spine surgery immediately. So I was bundled into *Ambulance #3* for the ride to a third hospital in Sacramento *where, I was told, my spine surgeon would meet me.*

The minute I arrived, I was whisked out of the ambulance, officially admitted to the hospital, given more tests, and the base of my skull was shaved in preparation for surgery. My sister Barbara said I was on the phone with her when they wheeled me into surgery and the last thing I said was, "I just want God to be glorified." I had *no idea* at that time how prophetic that pronouncement would be!

By surgery time, around 11:30 in the morning on July 12, I had had test after test at *three* different hospitals, and a "Mr. Toad's Wild Ride" of *three* ambulance trips and hospital visits stretching throughout the *very long* night.

When my spine surgeon, made his 12 inch long incision, he found a massive blood clot mysteriously enclosing several inches of my spinal column. He had no explanation as to why and how this had happened. His medical team was also mystified.

After a 5 ½ hour surgery in which the clot was scraped away and bone was shaved, I was finally able to see visitors in the recovery room. I don't recall much about this because by that time I hadn't slept for over 36 hours—except for my Morphine induced dozing and surgery nap. However, my husband told me that as I regained consciousness, I talked and laughed with family and friends, and everyone was very optimistic that everything was on course for a routine post surgery recovery.

In fact, for the next two days my behavior was normal and no one had any cause for alarm. There was even some discussion of my discharge in a few days.

Then on Monday July 15, the third day after my surgery, I could barely talk. My eyes continued to show recognition, but I struggled to form thoughts. My medical team was bewildered. I vaguely remember feeling terribly frightened.

July 16, four days after my surgery, my doctors decided that perhaps Dilaudid, a very powerful medication they had prescribed for my spine surgery pain, was the reason I was losing speech and cognitive function, so they discontinued it. I was left temporarily with only Norco. By Wednesday July 17, my husband reported that my eyes showed *only* intense pain.

Briefly and unexpectedly, on Thursday morning July 18, my speech suddenly improved. I was alert, wanted my hair washed, and a shower. Teresa, my daughter in law, helped me. I talked to my sisters on the phone. It seemed as if that, whatever breakdown had occurred, it was past.

However, later that evening, I lost speech capability once more. My eyes still showed that I recognized people and I could say a word here and there, but I couldn't finish a sentence. My son said I was visibly frustrated and confused. My sister Janice said she tried to talk to me on the phone, but my words made no sense at all.

By Friday July 19, my pain had become so horrible that my family reported that I was gnashing my teeth and thrashing about in agony. I remained incoherent and confused. I had become fearful of the medical staff and shrank in alarm when a new nurse came in to take care of me.

With my behavior becoming increasingly bizarre, my medical team decided to take away *all* pain medication except for occasional Tylenol. They were desperate for answers. I was in nightmarish pain.

By the evening of Friday July 19, 8 days after the 911 call, my paranoia, and confusion had become so great that I spit out *all* medication and would take *no* pills from the nurses. I thought they were trying to kill me. My husband faired only a little better in trying to help.

By Saturday July 20, I could not speak at all. *No words, period!*

Sunday July 21, I didn't recognize *anyone*—not my husband, my son, my daughter-in-law, nor my friends. I was totally disorientated, in unbearable pain, and inordinately afraid. My husband said I was acting so strangely that no one knew what to do.

Finally, nine days after my emergency surgery, the doctors decided to extract spinal fluid for further testing. Initially, every time they inserted the needle, they hit a rod or screw from the spinal fusion that almost fills my back from the tailbone to the Thoracic 10, as well as my neck—the result of breaking my back and neck in an auto accident years before, as well as severe scoliosis stenosis. Eventually, they were able to do an ultrasound. They hoped the test results would provide information that would help them identify effective strategies for my treatment.

On Monday July 22, there was no improvement in my condition. I was unconscious most of the time; delusional at other times. The doctors had begun to speculate about spinal meningitis, but they had no definite answers as yet. Blood tests were continued every few hours until I eventually had to have a port for injections and blood draws.

On Tuesday July 23, I remained unable to speak, but my actions indicated that I was hallucinating and terribly frightened.

Then... the test results came back. They decisively confirmed that I had "viral herpes simplex spinal meningitis." Mystified doctors told my husband that it was extremely rare and—the worst possible kind of meningitis. They said there was only a 1 in 500,000 chance of getting it. Doctors indicated that the virus must have entered my back during the hours it was open for spine surgery.

I became more and more ill—losing consciousness frequently, talking strangely if I spoke at all, and demonstrating bizarre personality characteristics. My physical body reacted ferociously as I bled internally, my legs became paralyzed, and I began to have seizures where my entire body shook violently and uncontrollably.

My status had gone from bad to worse... and then to desperate. My emergency spine surgery had morphed into an accumulation of very grave issues—which the doctors seemed to be powerless to control.

Finally, in a desperate attempt to save my life and my brain, my medical team prescribed drugs equivalent in strength to chemotherapy medication to be administered via IV for 14 days. Without this drug series, the doctors told my husband, my chances of dying were at least 70%. My husband decided the possible side effects were worth the risk—since saving my life was paramount.

At 7:30 AM on July 24, 13 days after my husband's 911 call, *I stopped breathing.* I was rushed to the Intensive Care Unit where they put me on a ventilator… and inserted breathing and feeding tubes. I was utterly helpless.

By that point in my illness, I had exhibited all of the worst symptoms of encephalitis except the most extreme: coma and… death. I had experienced respiratory failure, intellectual impairment, personality and mood changes, memory problems, leg paralysis, hearing deficits, loss of muscle coordination, excessive muscle and total body weakness and speech impairment. The result—according to medical experts—was that I would never be "normal" again.

But there was more to come… *I then went into a coma.*

My body and brain were shutting down.

My son strongly felt my coma was "God-induced" since the pain—with no relief from medication—had become unbearable.

The doctors all reported that they had never seen a case such as mine, where each new day brought devastating new health issues—that had no conclusive explanation and no effective treatment.

I remained in a coma on Thursday July 25.

I was still in a coma on Friday July 26. The medical staff was still "clueless," to quote my husband, about what they should do to make me better. Everything was experimentation.

Then Saturday July 27 came. My husband said that by that point, there was no life in my eyes, no recognition of anyone, and no sign of brain activity. I just stared. I could not speak… could not move. Even though my body was present, I remember nothing at all.

My youngest sister Janice reported that she and her husband arrived that night from Arizona. She said I was completely unresponsive to her or anyone else. She was stunned at seeing my lifeless looking body hooked up to a ventilator with a feeding tube running down my nose into my stomach. She was aghast that my body was so swollen that even my distended tongue protruded from the side of my mouth. I didn't look anything like the sister she knew and loved.

On Sunday July 28, I remained unconscious.

I was still comatose on Monday July 29.

On July 30, I continued to be completely unresponsive.

Yet, through all of this, *faith was still alive* as seen in my sister Janice's email to my family. She asserted that, "With God all things are possible, and I am expecting a miracle..." Other family and friends continued to pray earnestly for that miracle.

Faithful friends visited me again and again, week after week in the hospital, always praying and believing. One of them teased me later, saying that she had never visited anyone in the hospital as often as she did me. One daily visitor tried repeatedly to get me to communicate, to make me laugh, anything to get me to respond.

My husband, the hero of this calamity, spent 14-16 hours a day taking care of my medical issues, discussing symptoms and procedures with doctors, and making tough decisions about my treatment, all the while proclaiming to the medical staff—*with steadfast faith*—that I *would* live and that I *would* recover full brain function.

In the meantime, my son Jon researched every issue and more that was presented. He found that the doctors were *correct:* my situation was essentially hopeless in every way. Yet, in spite of that, he unwaveringly believed that God would intervene and do the *impossible.*

Not everyone believed. While in the ICU, in a coma, I couldn't breathe or eat on my own, so the doctors (five of them) recommended that my husband *strongly* consider taking me off the ventilator. They were adamant that I would not live long anyway. And, they warned, if by some chance I did live, with the dreadful effects of encephalitis, the possibility of my *ever* having *normal* brain function was *zero*. Most likely, I would have *minimal* cognitive ability.

As days passed, the doctors persisted in recommending that my husband approve removing the ventilator—letting me die sooner, rather than later. My husband's response was an unequivocal, *"No."*

Then, slowly… my oxygen count began to improve and finally, after about a week, I was able to breathe once again on my own. And, I was moved from the ICU to a regular hospital floor.

Eventually, after gradually struggling to open my eyes again and again, I could keep my eyes open, but I still couldn't talk.

Suddenly one day, completely out of the blue, I said a lot of words. They made no sense, but they were *words*.

Later, I started reading a few words from the ticker tape on the bottom of the TV screen—which everyone thought was very weird, since they didn't realize at first why I was saying such odd things in what they thought was response to their conversation.

I refused to eat hospital food because—in my still delusional state—I was afraid someone would poison me. Instead, I asked for bread with *lots* of butter from the Cheesecake Factory. My devoted husband complied—bringing me a huge container of butter and *lots* of bread. However, it didn't taste good after all! But, I *did* have *that container of Cheesecake Factory butter for a long time!*

I slept a lot during this time and hallucinated when I was awake. In time, my speech transitioned to where the few words I spoke were clearer, but they still made no sense: there was no context; and I couldn't form a sentence.

Then on Thursday, August 1, my blood pressure suddenly skyrocketed. I showed signs of cardiac distress so I was moved again—to the Cardiac Care Unit. After treatment, my blood pressure dropped to very dangerously low levels, but was finally stabilized.

Days passed in which I was still unconscious or semi-conscious.

More tests determined that my dopamine level was excessively high, making me see things that weren't there and afraid of everything.

Encephalitis raged.

I still didn't recognize anyone.

I didn't know where I was.

I thought people were trying to hurt me.

I said very strange things that no one could understand, and others that didn't remotely fit with who I was and how I thought.

I remained delusional for several more days.

Since the hospital staff's focus had been on saving my life, no one realized when exactly it happened, but somehow they had badly fractured *three* upper thoracic vertebras—increasing my already ghastly pain.

Yet, the nurses reported to my family that during some nights—all night long—I would say, "Thank you, Jesus!" "Thank you, Jesus!" crying out to the only Help I knew Who had the answers for my agony.

After about 10 days in the Cardiac Care Unit, my medical team decided they wanted to release me from the hospital. *They believed they could do nothing else for me* even though I was still very, very sick. I remained confused and exceptionally weak, and my husband and son vehemently disagreed with turning me out.

So… many long discussions and much research took place.

Through all of this, family and friends never stopped praying for a miracle of healing.

On August 8, my son posted the following on Facebook:

"Earlier this week she [Mom] woke up for about an hour and started putting together lots of little (mostly intelligible but out of context) sentences. That was encouraging. Since then she has been sleeping A LOT. The nurses aren't concerned because she wakes up when they call her. She is making slow progress with speech and physical therapy. Still hurts to eat. The doctors' threatened to send her to Eskaton (convalescent home) yesterday but Dave (and I) are adamantly opposing. My mom would freak out. She still needs to make significant progress with physical abilities before they move her to a rehab hospital. Last night the nurses said that the night before she just kept saying "Thank You Jesus" in her sleep… that is kind of cool…"

August 9 came—my birthday. It had been almost a month since my initial ambulance ride to the hospital. Everyone hoped that I would be well enough for the little birthday party they had planned by my hospital bed. However, I remained unconscious and remember nothing. The staff ate my cupcakes!

Then, on August 11, the physical therapist was successful in helping me to take steps. After that, my sister Janice posted, "Linda took six steps forward and six steps backward, and then sat down for a bit and did it again… with our God ALL THINGS ARE STILL POSSIBLE!"

Several days passed with little additional change and the doctors were increasingly insistent that my husband move me out of the hospital. They felt there would be little or no, further improvement. Therefore, as they saw it, *there was no point in my being there.* Their prognoses remained grim—but *they had no more ideas to try to help me.*

By August 18, my husband intensified his efforts to coordinate with the hospital to find a suitable place to move me to. He visited various rehab centers, trying to find the best place for my condition. My physical state continued to deteriorate from the effects of the encephalitis and many weeks in the hospital. I remained delusional. On August 20, when a scale was brought in, I thought they were trying to kill me.

Then… on August 22, my husband was told by hospital staff that I *would* be released that day—*like it or not!* By that time, my husband had learned that most rehab/skilled nursing facilities available through our insurance either wouldn't take me because of my condition, or were full. I ended up at a place that turned out to be one of the lowest rated rehab centers on the Kaiser list. It turned out *not* to be a good situation.

The rehab center staff was often very lax in their attention to providing essential care. However, it made me even more motivated to work as hard as possible to get better and get out of there. *I wanted to go home*—more than anything else! So I did everything I was told to do and more, to get stronger and to use my brain again. I had no appetite, but forced myself to eat. I struggled to use my walker to take steps, going from being so weak I could barely lift my light blanket to finally being able to take faltering baby steps. I spoke haltingly when I entered the facility; however, I passed every speech test, all tests of mental capability, and was even able to correct some mistakes in the testing system that the therapist had overlooked… in only a few days.

I was overjoyed to finally be *conscious* and to *participate* logically in conversations with my visitors! They reported my speech as hesitant at first, but improving exponentially every day. My brain so thoroughly healed that everyone—even the therapist doing the testing—totally marveled at my progress. I had 100% normal brain function within *seven weeks* of the dire prediction that it would take *at least a year or more* before I would regain—*if* I regained a small measure of brain function.

Through all of those days on end of agony, fear, and ravaged body—61 days—I nevertheless felt the comfort and peace of God's presence—somewhere deep inside my spirit—in the midst of my worst pain.

The truth is that God didn't stop the weeks of horrific, agonizing pain... of being in a coma, the loss of breathing function, paralysis, seizures, cardiac issues, terrible confusion and fear... no, not even the substandard treatment in the rehab center. He didn't keep my muscles from their frightening deterioration from the 61 days of lying flat on my back in bed unable to help myself. *He was with me through it all—* even when I was unconscious. As I regained awareness, I began to realize that God was powerful *in* my situation, and would *continue* to be with me *through* everything I faced—no matter how long it took or how hard it was.

I am forever grateful to my devoted husband who tirelessly advocated for me in the face of grim medical facts and doctors' declarations that he should prepare to bury me. His unwavering faith, one day at a time—and often one hour and one minute at a time—was nothing short of extraordinary. His and my son's rock solid bold faith—that I would get well, and be normal—no matter the medical prognoses, were nothing short of amazing.

Through it all, many friends continued to pray and visit. They earnestly hoped that their presence and their prayers would help bring me back to rational consciousness and health, even though it was very difficult, some later reported, to go against the doctors' advice to let me "go."

My family... *always* stood by me—asking and believing God for a miracle.

As for the doctors... they told me later that they simply did not *know* what to do. They had never seen a blood clot enclose a segment of spine before. They had no idea where the internal bleeding came from. And, after my sudden spine surgery, as the lethal spinal meningitis caused encephalitis, they watched in shock as my symptoms became life-threatening and debilitating, spiraling completely out of control, with no answers and no visible signs for hope. They gave up on me.

I finally came home on September 9th—two days short of nine weeks from that fateful July day when this saga began. I cried with joy and gratitude. Still weak as a newborn kitten, but overwhelmed by God's mercy and grace that had restored me to that point; Hopeful and expectant that I would continue to get much, much better.

On Oct. 21, 2013, my son wrote a fitting summary on Facebook:

"Just over three months ago my mom was rushed to the Emergency Room in Sacramento. Over the course of the next several weeks her condition deteriorated. Doctors identified that a virus was attacking her brain and spine. She eventually fell into a coma and the doctors, despite their most drastic treatment measures, believed that she would not make it (all five of them). Her "best case scenario" was that if she came out of it she would have severe brain damage and recovery (at best 70 or 80 percent) would take a year or many years. The team of doctors prompted us to make decisions and arrangements to prepare for her death.

Last night we all went out to the Cheesecake Factory for dinner. She is 100% mentally and cognitively recovered. We could not have imagined in our boldest prayers such a quick and complete recovery. We are so thankful for all of your prayers and encouraging words. We are so thankful to have my mom back and trusting God for a complete physical recovery. We are blessed…"

The surgeon who performed my emergency spine surgery told me six months afterwards, "*You are a miracle!*" He continued, "I know it's strange for *me* to say that [since doctors' deal in science and facts], but it's true… I could easily count on one hand the times I've seen anything like what happened to you. It's [your recovery is] miraculous."

Although there were no viable solutions from medical science, God intervened. There was *nothing* I could do to help myself since I was mostly unconscious, and desperately, hopelessly ill. But with

God... *nothing* is impossible. I am alive; my brain is 100% restored; I am regaining physical strength daily—and I am so deeply, humbly thankful.

I experienced in the most personal way that even in the darkness of unbearable pain and deadly diseases, *God was always there, with me ...* even "through the valley of the shadow of death".

"Even though I walk through the valley of the shadow of death, I will fear no evil, for You are with me . . ." **Psalm 23:4 (NIV)**

Save Him
By
Brittany Hill

You look at him, then at the Most High then him again,
Realizing how after he has defiled you
He is the one?
You can hear a soft chuckle in your subconscious
God is tickled by your fantasy
But you know the real truth
He is only here to fulfill his fleshy desires.
I can save him. He's lukewarm
He just needs a little bit of guidance
While he uses you up
Drying you like an old woman with fifty cats
It has made you into a human hoarder
Carrying all of his useless crap
Is he washed in the blood?
Does he fast when called?
He does know what fasting is, right?
I can save him
Well maybe next week he might want to come to church
Sending you all types of flags that go unnoticed
My baby is a ride or die, real hood type, busting on these niggas for me
Oh really?
What have you subjected yourself to?
Living a fake Cinderella story
Charming you right out of your panties
Is he going to love you through your hurt and the pain?
Love you unconditionally through thick and thin before the lust began
And love your ten kids like next of kin
Child please he will be gone before the wind
The Raiders will win a Super Bowl before he will stay
All your friends saying you need to let of these little boys and get you a real man
Living in a house like Sodom and Gomorrah
Desperately looking for the attention of love
Aren't you tired of the constant digging for lust?
The Bible says he who finds a wife finds a good thing
The key point is that we are to wait on God
Walk with God and in due time he will supply all the desires of your heart

Plant Me on Higher Ground
By
Dana D'Amico

Hardships often prepare ordinary people, for an
extraordinary destiny...

C.S. Lewis

Growing up, I can only remember so much of my childhood. Not understanding some things and always feeling like I had to participate in activities to be accepted. As an adult, I can now go back in time and remember the unconscious state of mind I was living in. It scares me to know I lived more than half of my life in a complete state of denial and emptiness, an emptiness that only other survivors could possibly understand.

I today, am in love with who I am and realize all of the wonderful things I could have accomplished if it hadn't been for the unselfish sickness of others contaminating my life. I go through bouts of anger, depression, darkness and times of extreme sadness that I recall from almost ten years ago.

Being on the constant battlefield of abusive relationships, I did whatever it took to try and get the love I wanted from individuals that were completely incapable of loving someone to begin with. Loving sick people doesn't make you healthier at all. I went on for years trying to fix everyone I spent time around when the fixing that needed to take place was in my own heart, mind and soul the entire time. I was the person that needed to be healed.

I remember back in elementary school my kindergarten teacher tying my tooth to a door and then slamming it shut to rip out one of my first teeth. Today that teacher would be put in jail for abuse. I can recall another teacher, Mrs. Little John who I adored and loved. She was so much fun, like another mom in my life; a loving, kind and amazing teacher. We painted and made crafts in kindergarten but the saddest thing is other than that, I only remember the traumatic parts. The memories returned to me when a therapist helped me deal with the agony and dysfunction I went through as a child and I learned to work through the pain and anger. It is daily work in process.

I always did well in art and writing but when it came to comprehending math, science and other subjects, I lacked the ability to keep hold of the materials I needed to complete tasks. It appeared that I had comprehension issues as I couldn't retain a lot of information at once. I recall falling asleep a lot. I know today it was most likely due to the fact that I was molested during my childhood from about the age of six, until I was nine years old.

Most of my childhood memories are gone, which has been confirmed by countless therapy sessions. I know today, at the age of 42, that there are blank spaces of my life that I just have to work though, I am only allowed snapshots. We have to remember that even though God protects us from evil things in life, the abuse we endure at the hands of our abusers will still attempt to kill our heart and rob us of our innocence. I know now that our brain actually protects us from wicked memories but they can come back to haunt you later in your teenage or adult years. Being transparent in my life today is what has made me heal and become stronger.

A majority of abusers were abused themselves, so I found myself doing the most profound thing almost a year and a half ago and actually giving God that burden and giving my abuser mercy. What I have to say is, for those out there who cry out and have pain they can't explain, get ready to dig deep because God wants you to have a pure heart and he will take you on a purely enlightening journey. I am a walking testimony.

Now at this point in my life I have come to question things in a completely different sense than before. I have learned to educate myself from a psychological standpoint. After four years of classes and education on sex trafficking and rape victimization, I can go through the pain with dignity. You mean to tell me I'm actually not a crazy person? I have seen case studies from neurological standpoints that actually show frontal lobe damage in children that have been molested or sexually abused. I find it absurd that today, we have this technology yet we don't utilize the assistance this could give to help with child development and abused victims as it would cost our medical industry too much money. If cases are identified early on we can take more preventative measures to avoid future issues.

I went through so much growing up thinking I was challenged and different from everyone else. What troubles me now, from my experience is the vast amount of individuals have endured trauma and continue to live in pain and darkness because they feel they don't have a choice or are too ashamed of the circumstances. I have walked through years of this mindset, thinking I had no purpose. Walking around like a zombie ready to lose my mind. I always felt no matter what I did, it wasn't enough, not a healthy state of mind at all. Like a leaf in the wind blowing out of control in all directions.

My life started with and ran into all sorts of addiction fazes. I went through years of simply making bad choices and loving the wrong people. Accepting what I thought was love because of the awful things that took place. I know this is tough for some to see and to hear, the transparency, but the secrets in my heart, mind and soul almost killed me several times. Too many times in my life I endangered myself because of abusive people treating me unbearably. If your innocence was taken at an early stage in life you mistake sex and other bad things as love. It is labeled as trauma bonding and it's a sick relationship that builds between abused individuals and their abuser.

We have to see in life that once an abuser is perpetrated there are automatic behaviors that take place and will continue if the abuse is never stopped. If the abusing takes place from ancestor to ancestor and is hidden time after time then it doesn't stop. A child will continue to lead a life of associating sex, secrets and other bad things to equate to "love" throughout their teenage and adult years. The same behaviors are passed down from generation to generation. These are situations and behaviors in life that are seldom discussed and I can say truthfully, have lead to my downfalls. No one realizes the battle that I had to fight for almost 30 years.

To go through a life, dark and unknown is just not acceptable. Remembering bits and pieces of the irregular patterns of my pain and childhood was so profound to me now. My innocence was taken as a child. My adolescent and teen years were hard to bear but if I continued to hold on to this bondage in my life, I would be doing God an injustice, let alone an injustice to others crying out for help.

I understand the fear. I can understand the scary parts now and can bear the pain, realizing that it's okay to shed a tear or two or even to just break down entirely. I have to share my story because if I don't, I won't heal. Recalling dire points are essential. Your healing and acceptance of the dark places of where you've been are so crucial to accepting who you truly are today. I have to recall the past to know where I came from. First step into living is forgiving yourself and the others who harmed you. God loved me unconditionally and moved me forward in life with power, strength and courage. Courage is what helps me share my journey. Courage and strength are what empower me. God's healing grace over my life and my downfalls is what pulled me through the dark pivotal times in my life. You must surrender your life and your will over to God. Not a day goes by that I'm not thankful for the life I am living today. He has removed the shame, sleepless nights and the pain. Nobody can love you greater that God. The memories of all those unpleasant things get less and less painful.

Recalling those dark places still happen occasionally. Remembering small pieces of memories is strange to me. It's not normal that the simple memory of black velvet wallpaper adorned with red can lead me back to a completely dreadful situation. It was a whole life of crazy experiences. It was being babysat by an adult that was bipolar and did not so great things to kids. Through many days of writing therapy I was able to sort out things that as I've become older, I can acknowledge and know they were not acceptable. Some people need to realize that all parents don't raise their kids the same way your own parents would. I've learned that there are sick people everywhere and secrets remain in all sorts of places. Abuse and life challenges do not discriminate. It's unreal that that wallpaper and memory can take me to a situation that, as a child, I shouldn't remember. Reliving experiences has been painful but has given me back my freedom of living. God has now taken away the pain but growing up was tough. Growing up, I was always looking for acceptance from whatever I could find. New friends, new life, new things, nothing pleased me because I was empty inside from all the pain.

The black velvet walls were the first thing I could recall from a therapy session. It started with the memory of Howdy Doody and black horned-rimmed glasses. I can now recollect who that person is and what that person did in my life. This therapist, at the time I thought was nuts but now I know the benefit of the writing that came from it. Then there was another dark place called rehab. Rehab was the best thing that could have ever happened in my life and I'm not embarrassed to say if I could check out for 30 days a year I would, to regroup, refocus and heal from life in general and the sick cultures that have ruined our society. There are ill people everywhere who most of all need to know they didn't become sick on their own.

I continue to write today and can see how this kind of creative therapy has helped me grow as a person. I continue to have brief moments of clarity. I can remember the little black dog that captivated a lot of my childhood. Her name was Pepper and I can recall, more than once, that little dog going after people that would try to come on my bed if I was tucked in at night. An animal can detect fear from a child and I think back now, as an adult, that she was always on my bed. She protected my heart and as a child, didn't realize it but now all grown up, I understand and it makes perfect sense.

Little things trigger the mind to see and feel these bad memories and they come back with a vengeance. They sneak up on you like sharp daggers and it pierces your heart to relive those awkward moments. This dog gave me the first unconditional love and with her and my sister around I felt safe. I can remember always wanting to sleep with my sister or with my parents and now that I'm older, I know why. Not anyone knew about this until I was an adult, after years of therapy. My parents just thought I wanted to be in their room all the time but now I know the reason why I made my bed beside them every night. I didn't want to be alone.

I spent a majority of my life in fear but survived it all. Knowing that I, myself was harmed and other kids are abused on a daily basis breaks my heart. Parents need to listen to their children and be aware because you might not be disturbed but there are a lot of sick people out there including those who could be family members, friends, teachers, business people and all shapes, sizes and likings. Sickness doesn't discriminate. I know it's hard to stomach but it is the truth in most cases. You have to go down memory lane of all the times things didn't seem right.

My sessions of therapy would always help me to remember triggers. My therapist would say one thing and then late that night I would end up writing things down. I would remember the girls at the house where I was being babysat talking about touching themselves and their private parts as a child. I know now, this wasn't right at all and did I go home and tell my mother? Of course not because those things were naughty and you don't tell secrets. How is it that the abusers can live their lives this way? They are able to because they are going through life unfixed just like I was at one point. You live in shackles and bondage until you ask God to remove the wrongs that have been created in your life. You put those things at the foot of the cross and ask God to take every inch of pain away. No one can understand the darkness unless they were an actual victim of the same pain. A darkness that is unfathomable unless you have actually lived it. I can't tell you how much I am thankful for. Continuously hiding the pain even as a child was so hard and I experienced so many things. Sometimes I can't imagine why God brought me through it all.

Some things I only remember because people have told me and through therapy. I often had negative thoughts. So many times I thought there were things wrong with me and I listened to others tell me there were things wrong with me. Due to always feeling insecure I tore myself apart. I had no self esteem and seemed to attract the people who would end up tearing me down more. I seemed to gravitate to whoever made me feel good and most of the time it was only to feel as if I belonged. I seemed to attach myself to anything but my own heart. I was constantly looking for acceptance. Even trying to be perfect for my parents when all along I was already perfect for my parents, I just never felt that way. I felt like nothing was ever good enough. I thrived as a dancer in high school and excelled at sports always getting complimented but that still wasn't enough. I can even say I did things at school that I knew I shouldn't just so I would be accepted by students and friends, because I was lost and in desperate need of validation.

Striving for acceptance, I did whatever it took to get or be loved. Having your virginity taken from you as a child is a horrific experience and can lead to so much heartache later in life. I'm a living testimony of the textbook study of the child, teen and adult that faced addiction and stormy times with unworthiness and self hatred. You become a ticking time bomb ready to explode.

School wasn't easy for me I had issues because my grades were not optimal but I would still make it through. I wasn't able to comprehend certain things due to the fact that all my energy was spent trying to block out fear yet still being afraid on a daily basis. I lived through life blinded by fear, agony and tears of impurity. I didn't stand up for myself because I never knew who I truly was until about four years ago. I finally learned to love me. It was a hard way to live and I kept those who should have been closest to me, at a distance.

I remember doing things in elementary school that were artistic. I loved my third grade teacher because we painted ceramics and I got to have fun and create through art. I always excelled in the subject because it helped to block things out and kept my mind busy. Art took away the pain and dancing made me feel like I was talented and special. There are proven points in neurology and brain activity that art and music can help produce healthy bonds within the mind that actually heal parts of the brain that deal with trauma.

There are case studies that show swelling in areas of the brain where the effects of trauma can be detected. Today's studies show frontal lobe damage to abused children or trauma victims. In our current era we have technology that can detect the damage at early stages so that a person doesn't have to self destruct from the abuse or molestation if treated properly by the correct professionals. It's almost impossible to understand what it does to a child during those years of maturity and growing up. Trauma, even to an adult can cause intense and irreversible damage without proper help or assistance.

I understand it because in my life, I walked through it. I walked the journey of addiction, abusive relationships and family turmoil. Even coming from a loving family didn't stop the pain. I love my family and I am who I am today because of what they instilled in me. My mother taught me to fight and fight hard. She made her struggle look easy but the only reason she made it through her storm was because of God's love. My mother is a masterpiece, of one of his miracles. I know today, that if she didn't make it through her storm I wouldn't be here to share this story.

I can attest to the miracle that God worked in my life ten years ago. My journey had only begun when my mother almost died of an aneurysm and stroke. She was on her path to recovery when two weeks later she became a widow. We lost my dad and then my whole world crumbled. I begin in this manner to give you a bare prefix of the pain and also to help me come to terms with my circumstances through writing this. This has been a true journey. I endured so much at once, that reliving the pain and agony of my child hood trauma as an adult has taken me down some painful paths to recovery. The loss and pain was dark and miserable but today, the healing has given me an abundant gratefulness to be standing, living, breathing and able to tell this story.

Within about 60 days my life was rocked and turned upside down. I was told by a doctor that I was lucky to be alive. Let me remind you, there were a lot of drunken nights where I was totally oblivious due to amount of drugs I was taking. I mastered the technique of managing prescription and other recreational drugs to alter my mental state depending on how I wanted to feel. Into about a month of my mother's recovery, I began having recollections and dreams of another night in my life that had been buried deep. The trauma of my past and the strain of both parents getting exceedingly ill at the same time put my heart and mind into a tailspin. I had to come to terms with the fact that I was sicker than I realized. Losing my father put me in a horrific state. It was this shock that triggered my agony as a child, teen and brought to the surface additional adult memories. I relived a dream every night after my father died that ended up setting me on the path to pursue therapy in order to get to where I am today and be able to share my story.

At the age of 19 I was raped. Raped by five men and you can only imagine what that was like. It was horrifying and every time I feel asleep for almost a year and a half after the occurrence, I relived that night. I remember going out with one of my best friends, whose name I choose to have remain anonymous through this journey to spare them the ordeal. Though I have made to decision to re-count my journey doesn't mean the other person has to. The constant anxiety and the acts I performed were unbearable. I drank from the about the age of 15 or 16 onward in attempts to bury the experience of rape, molestation and abusive sexual relationships. Sex was love to me, if you gave sex that meant you would get love in return. The night of the rape I was drugged by something that had been put in my drink. I can now recall these things due to the effects of PTSD, having to endure the suffering of my mother and then agony of my father's death. Trauma can trigger pretty specific memories. The unremitting nightmares were the breaking point and through therapy and the friendships built, I have found the strength to heal through those circumstances.

Through my teenage and adult years I found myself continuously in abusive relationships. Why, because abuse was love to me. I went through life drinking and partying because it was the accepted thing to do. Knowing what I know today, I realize how lucky I am to be alive. The 60 days checking in and out of hospitals and undergoing 24 hours surveillance were insane.

During the process of almost losing my mother and the actual passing of my father, there was also a disturbance in my own home. My fiancé of 10 years, at the time was also physically abusive. That night in April of 2004 was a complete nightmare. Two times prior, I had almost committed suicide from taking the drug that the hospital had prescribed. I drank myself into oblivion numerous times to hide the pain and darkness I was desperately trying to avoid and I had no explanation why. Waking up in the hospital twice with security checking on me and being on a 48 hour watch trying to decipher the reason for my self destruction was crazy.

I can recall my ex hovering over me asking me what was wrong with me, when the whole time he was wrong for me and sick himself. He led my family to think he was taking care of me when in actuality he was abusing me, mentally and physically. No one knew because I was too scared to tell anyone. I was living my entire dysfunctional life in secrecy. Not only was I taking the prescriptions for my mental stability, I was drinking and using other recreational drugs I shouldn't have been mixing with the medications.

The week of April 2004 got only worse after a weeklong drinking binge and mixing prescription drugs. Not to forget the additional drug that my ex would place in my drink without my knowledge. I was suffering total black outs, having memory lapses and then I caught my ex cheating on me. That night, he furnished me with a lethal dose of a liquid drug, I can't recall the name they listed in the toxicology reports but was told based on the dosage I could have died. He ended up throwing me against a wall which resulted in me blacking out. The next morning I awoke in a padded room at Placer County Jail, not even knowing why I was there. Bruised and badly beaten I was told by the police sergeant what had transpired and they wanted to know if I wanted to press charges against my finance. I asked what for. They proceeded to tell me that the police had been called because a neighbor heard yelling and a commotion. That was the most unbearable time in my life, facing my family, asking them to come and pick me up from jail and not being able to explain to them what happened.

I went back to my house I first bought, which was a beautiful 4 ½ bedroom home with a pool and everything you could dream of. In two weeks my home was ruined due to drugs, alcohol and the effects of an abusive relationship. I was scared and afraid he would hurt me again. I called two friends of mine and in two weeks, walked away from it all. Alive, scared and crazily thinking I was going to jail for harming a police officer the night he had beaten me. The drug he had placed in a drink he gave me left me with no memory of actually harming anyone. I will say that I had God watching over me the entire time. I chose to go to rehab after a 4th attempt of killing myself while at my mothers. I remember the night I told one of my best friends, that if she didn't come and get me then, that I wouldn't be there the next day.

I made the best decision of my life at that time, choosing to surrender and give it all to God. I cried for days, non-stop. I decided to go to a woman's program for almost 3 months and it was the best thing I could have done for myself, my family and all my friends that I hurt in the process. I can recall about a month into rehab, walking into a church of which I'm currently still a member and let me tell you, without all these people in my life, I would not be the woman I'm proud of being today. There are men and woman in this church that remain persistent in teaching me to let God have it all and let God love me for me. To all of the women and men who poured into my life from COP, you changed my life forever. I am a brave woman of God and I can say today, I love Dana D'Amico.

It has been hard, rough and scary at times but I have learned to not sweat the small things in life because God has that all covered. He has me covered in his abundant light and love. Now I can share my story to help others feel their way through the darkness. I'm a writer, dancer choreographer, life mentor, am living dreams I thought I never would and with that I'm so honored to walk through Gods journey with joy. Joy in my heart that no other can replace or ever take away from me.

I was a victim for years and today I'm a survivor. I know through all the sickness and turmoil that God was building me up the entire time. Through the sleepless nights, the coma induced drug nights and all the nights I could have died, God brought me through to carry out this message for other woman enduring their own battles. I am a woman of freedom, no longer a victim and am in love with me today. God will show you the way if you allow him to heal you. My story is dark but now there is nothing but light shining on those horrible days I lived through. God has planted me on higher ground and living through him is the path that I will continue on. He has placed wonderful men in my life as friends and those men know who they are. Four years ago they changed my life. In fact, on my 40th birthday, they spoke life back into this heart and this journey is only beginning.

So for all of you that are suffering from the sickness of guilt, pain and turmoil, this is to let you know that there is a life of bliss and true happiness out there for you. I'm living it. God has placed me on a higher ground to live out His word and to carry others to the cross to be delivered from harm, pain and discouragement. God, you have put me exactly where you wanted me and without all the people that helped build me up through the process, I wouldn't be the woman I am today. God you have sustained me and I will continue to carry your message. I want others to know that their pain can dissipate and they can live a normal life no matter the trials and tribulations they have endured. Nothing comes easy and life is a daily work in progress. I work hard every day but the rest of my worries and hardships I have given to God to work out as He sees fit. I'm approaching my 11th year of sobriety and I'm proud to be healthy and drug free. No prescription or recreational drugs only Gods holy spirit living and breathing inside and out of my heart daily.

If you don't want to be scared anymore and you want to experience the life that I live, well get ready to be filled with the one and only drug, the Holy Spirit and the blood of Jesus because today, that is what keeps me safe and in good hands. God holds me in his arms daily, every hour and second of my life and I wouldn't have it any other way. Take me to my path of a higher ground because my life has only just begun. I live through you and on a daily basis, will try to improve myself and others for the rest of my life. I'm planted on a higher ground and protected from my past and I'm not going anywhere until God takes me away. Thank you to all the people in my life that have poured into me. This was only one storm He has seen me through. I still have troubles but get through them much easier with prayer and the help of others. Your storm is your story. Don't be afraid to walk through them because what lies on the other side is the story that God has already written for you.

Life will plant you on higher ground when you least expect it. Enjoy the ride because there is nowhere else I'd rather be. Be blessed and loved by others. My feet and my footprints were planted for a purpose which is Gods purpose, not my own. Today, I see my dreams unfolding and I know that I have not gotten here on my own accord. Remember God has your dreams in his hands but it is up to you to listen, to hear his word and follow His direction. Being obedient is a work in progress and removing your flesh is a daily process. Take each day one day at a time and your blessings will unfold. I'm right where I need to be and it is so refreshing to my heart to finally be able to say… I love me, unconditionally.

Anna Marie

Comes the Dawn
By
Kelly Freeman

Comes the dawn and she's still glowing
Glowing from the ceremony
Glowing from the bridegrooms kiss
Glowing from the reception
Glowing, but not knowing

Not knowing that the moment he leaves to get ice
He's making phone calls to the girl he met in the lobby
When they checked in
Not knowing that she's kissing the residue of the
Other woman's lip-gloss
Not knowing, not knowing
But still glowing
And then comes the dawn

Comes the dawn and she rolls over
Kisses him good morning
Makes him breakfast
Sends him off to work
And she's beaming
She's beaming, and he's scheming
Scheming to meet up with a girl he met at the gym
See if he can get a little trim
It's not that he isn't getting it at home.
Just his voracious appetite selfishly getting the better of him
Now Wifey's calling

Calling to see if he'll be late again
And see if she should keep dinner warm for him
When he comes home bearing the scent of another woman's skin
He won't come home, but he will call
Say that he got drunk at the bar
Pulled over and fell asleep in his car all night
(Raised voice in question)

All night?!
And they'll fight and they'll fight
Fight until blood fills the air
Until she's washing glass fragments out of her hair
From the window he shoved her into

Tablespoons of Tears

Fight until her knuckles are scraped
Bones are broken, and fingers are taped
No officer it wasn't rape, sometimes we role play
And then comes the dawn

Comes the dawn and he's bearing gifts
Making up, kissing busted lips.
And now he's smiling
He's smiling
Smiling as he redirects phone bills, credit card receipts, and lies
Smiling while he hides porn, massage bills
And homemade sex tapes of his lovers
Smiling as he enters her as if he loves her
Injecting her with the same poison
That is secretly killing him
And then comes the dawn

Comes the dawn and she realizes she isn't the one
Realizes that although she's done
Everything required of her, met every need
And fulfilled every tasteless fantasy
She's not enough
She realizes he's toxic and hazardous
3 blood tests later she's positive that
She's not positive and she's happy
And then comes the dawn

Comes the dawn and they're dressed to the nines
She's in her little black dress he's wearing his favorite red tie
And they're close
The car pulls up but he doesn't get the door
She figures it's cool I'll let it slide once more.
She's too happy to be deterred
And they ride
They ride until they reach their destination
To him it's no big deal, but for her a vacation
And she's basking
They arrive and she says
This is all for you
The flowers, the friends your whole family
I asked the same man that married us to perform the Eulogy
I hope you like it, because I like it
Yeah, she liked it.

Childhood Tears, Adult Fears, Victory Cheers
By
Denice Jones

There is no greater agony than bearing an untold story
inside you.

Maya Angelou

Anna Marie

Friday, October 25, 2013

Dressed in my Sunday clothes, I was headed out the door to the funeral of a childhood neighbor. Shaken, I stopped at the doorway, turned around and rushed over to sit down at my computer. Nothing felt right about me going to the funeral, nothing. Tears began to fall, massive shoulder shaking and stomach hurting tears. I began to imagine talking to his parents, then his sisters and brothers, screaming at the top of my voice. "Today is the day my childhood neighbor, your son and your brother, is being laid to rest and *he* was my molester!"

My parents were the founders of two black social clubs in the suburb of Sacramento, Colonial Heights which was best known as Oak Park, where most of the population was mostly Black, Latino and Asian. Most of us who grew up in the area, didn't know that the neighborhood playground and park were named after the McClatchy family who originally owned the land. The McClatchy family donated most of their property to be enjoyed by its multi-cultural residents. McClatchy Park was where we played in the toddler pool and an adult swimming pool. I still remember playing in the toddler pool as a small child, a very pleasant memory as I loved being in water. I had always imagined living under the water in a house with my family.

Growing up in the area, we had a bag lady that stood on the corner of Broadway and Sacramento Blvd. She would give the neighborhood kids each a dollar to buy ice cream from Red Fox, the local liquor store located on what was then named Sacramento Blvd but now has been renamed Martin Luther King Blvd. Later as a teenager, I found out she was the daughter of the very wealthy McClatchy family. She was picked up daily by a limousine from her corner at the end of her day, always returning in the early morning, again giving out dollars to the neighborhood kids. She was never harmed although she lived her adult life on the streets. The people of

Oak Park respected and cared for her because she loved Oak Park and its neighborhood kids. She set it up in her will that McClatchy Park could never be sold after her family ended up selling part of the land to the McGeorge School of Law. McGeorge tried to buy the park for a parking lot but failed. She, being the last of the McClatchys denied their request, blocking anyone from selling, demolishing or using it for any other purpose than entertaining the locals.

Family lawyers hired to help her maintain her finances while living her pauper lifestyle, tried to have her committed because of her way of life, attempting to find her too incompetent to handle her family businesses. Oak Park gathered in prayer and sat in at her trials giving character witness to how loving, caring and responsible she was, explaining to the courts how she loved the park and the kids. She was always clean and well groomed but wore old clothes as she spent her time and money giving to charities that cared for families. She was found competent and lived in peace until her death. Oak Park loved her and they showed it by caring for her.

The two black social clubs formed by my parents were The Royal Twelve, created to socialize twelve married couples who lived in the area and The Starlite Jets which allowed their single friends to join in the fun of dancing the night away. Mom loved to dance. My parents and their friends held society balls and partied nearly every weekend. Not complaining, it was the most exciting part of my childhood! My mother would dress up in the most beautiful formal gowns and Daddy had tuxedos, more than one and they modeled before my siblings and I. Each of us cheered and praised them as they sashayed out the front door. My molester then came in to stay with us until they returned. My bed time was soon to become the most traumatic experience of my life.

We needed a sitter when Daddy and Mommy went out and he was chosen to watch us, as he was one of the oldest teenagers in our neighborhood. Named after his father, he was the oldest of ten and we called him Harry. He, at the age of about thirteen or fourteen years old became our sitter. His younger sister was the oldest girl and was expected to stay home to watch her five younger siblings while his mother went out and socialized which she did more often than not. The oldest girl of the ten seldom played with us as she spent most of her time in her room writing in her journals. She grew up to be a local area play write and became very popular, producing many plays that were enjoyed by all who supported her.

We never wanted for anything. Daddy, an ex-military army man, turned Communications Specialist Supervisor was the first black man to work at the Travis Relay Communications Station in Davis, California. Mother, a very successful and popular entrepreneur, owned her own beauty salon named Eva's Beauty Nook located behind the local barber shop on Stockton Boulevard in Oak Park.

It was on their party nights that my parents stayed out late and Harry would send us to bed as soon as they left out the door. He would separate me from my sister, making me lie in my parent's bed. My brothers were sent to the loft room upstairs and my sister was sent to our room down the hall. I remember trying to resist going in my parent's room but my sister liked having the bed to herself and urged me to go lay in their bed. The thing I remember most was the comfort I felt from sleeping on my Daddy's side of the bed. Being a Daddy's girl was how I made it through this experience. He helped me develop confidence, a confidence that was soon to be challenged over and over again.

Fully clothed, Harry would make me lie on my stomach while he climbed on top of me, pressing, grinding and pushing himself into my backside. Hours would pass when then he tried to make me do the same. Becoming angry because I was too little to press hard enough to satisfy him, he would angrily roll me off of him and jerk me back on my stomach to continue what he was doing. I became afraid of him. Harry would turn me on my back and push himself between my legs pressing into my pelvis and I didn't understand what was happening.

One night he tried to penetrate me but stopped when I squirmed in discomfort. I remember him talking to himself about the pain it was causing me and he was afraid the others would hear my cries. He began covering my mouth so my siblings would not find out but that made it difficult for me to breathe. I remember telling him to leave me alone because I was sleepy; begging him to please let me go to sleep. Harry, unable to achieve satisfaction, would turn me back on my stomach, grinding into me again until he would fall asleep on top of me for hours at a time. After this I became restless and agitated when I would get sleepy, sometimes nearly screaming to be left alone so I could sleep. Thus my mom started calling me mean and irritable. Something had to be on my back to help me calm down. I would put my pillow on my back to cover me and then fall off to sleep. When I got older and for many years after, whenever I saw him, I would hold my breath while in his presence. This happened up until the last time I saw him on my front porch when my daughter was just three.

In 1995, my youngest brother was released from prison after six years of incarceration. Harry came by when he found out he was home and living with me at our Grandma's house. My daughter and I were preparing to leave to go to church and we heard voices. I recognized Harry's by his distinctive laughter which his whole family shared. I held my breath, almost panicking as I thought of a way to protect her from him. Walking to the front door I pulled my daughter to my side and continued out onto the porch. Quickly, I moved passed my brother to the first step, but he in a raised voice, called me by my childhood name, Denny, asking who it was that I was holding hands with. My brother told him it was my daughter. He then asked loudly "Denny is that your daughter? You said you were never having children!"

My brain was rattled with that statement. I couldn't believe he remembered me saying that. So he also must have remembered molesting me. Moving down the steps quickly I kept looking back to see if he was following me. He wasn't but his eyes kept looking at my daughter. I ran with her in my arms to my car, praying that he would not be there when we got back.

When we returned he was gone and it was nearly ten years before I would see him again. All I can do is thank God for protecting my daughter. I lay in bed holding her after reading her a story and remembered how grateful to God I was for making me a mother. No longer fearful about being violated in the night, my mind drifted back to when we started out our life together, as mother and daughter.

After God blessed me to be the mother of a three day old girl, our journey as a first time mom with a newborn, started out with a serious challenge. I couldn't touch her to clean her properly. I thought I was molesting her every time I bathed her. Giving her a bath was so emotional that I would cry as I avoided washing or even getting close to her private area. My attempts to clean her consisted of sprinkling water on her private area, therefore avoiding skin contact.

Due to my fear of bathing her completely, she soon developed a rash and I had to take her to the pediatrician. The nurse practitioner told me she had a yeast infection. What? How did she get that when I did not touch her in that area? That was when the practitioner told me I needed to clean her thoroughly and showed me how to do it properly. When we got home I prayed to God to help me overcome this problem and take care of this baby like I should.

As if God said I was not alone, two popular talk shows in the same week had four couples in which the wives and mothers were having the same issue with changing and bathing their newborns. One couple was devastated because the mother could not change a diaper. Her husband had to leave work to come home to bathe and change the baby. I, almost in tears, listened as they described how the women were molested as children by family or friends of their family. The molestations left them mentally paralyzed and unable to properly care for their babies.

Noticing the women on the talk show who were molested were successful business women before even having their first baby. They too stated they did not fit in. I felt I did not fit in because of my early physical development and also had no one to talk to about this problem. They thought they were becoming mentally ill, off balance and unstable. The husbands had nowhere to turn to for help and were depressed. Scared to leave their child alone with its mother, some even contemplated divorce and getting sole custody of the child. There was so much pain in the eyes of these husbands who were desperately trying to understand the trauma their wives had suffered at the hands of a stranger the husbands never knew. This person took a piece of their wife's life and they had no idea how to fix it or how to get that piece back.

Feeling their pain because I too had thought I may have a mental illness due to the hand of the molester, someone whom I knew. Deciding at a very young age not to be sexually active, I did not see myself able to be in love. Love was a foreign word and it had lost meaning with me. Outside of the family, I found it difficult to love others but I knew how to tolerate another person. Smiling and making people laugh was a very natural act for me but when it got too personal, I would usually walk away from the relationship.

On the talk show I saw how desperate they were to seek help with their problem. They got the help by a psychologist appointed to them. I sought help through studying the Bible which was my constant companion, guiding me on living a successful Christian life. I learned to listen to the quiet voice of the Holy Spirit comforting me. The Holy Spirit taught me how to hold the baby and burp her.

She was hard to burp due to issues that occurred during her birth. The Holy Spirit told me that I was loved and would very soon overcome this affliction of not being able to bathe this innocent infant. That night I bathed my daughter for the first time without any fear. I cleaned her thoroughly, applying the ointment to cure the infection and told her that I was going to protect her from ever being touched by anyone improperly.

A strong sense of protection came over me and I knew I would no longer have an issue, the problem was gone. Yet the issues of the my molestation made me unable to trust people and I put up walls basically keeping to myself and only getting out with my baby to go to church or shopping. Music, primarily singing became my refuge. I did a lot of singing in church as my social outing but would afterwards go home and shut down. I immersed myself in being the best mom I could be and at helping my baby develop normally. I handled every test and trial that came with the help of faithful church friends and family. There was no one I could talk to about my molestation so I leaned on the only one I could trust, God and His still comforting voice. I learned to hear, obey and believe that everything would be alright.

Ten years passed. While at the church, my refuge in the midst of a storm of depression and confusion, we were asked to write on a piece of paper forgiveness for a person who hurt us in our past. Instructed to do this on that night in the Singles Ministry was very challenging, for the past ten years I had suppressed the molestation, never revealing to anyone how it had affected me emotionally. Although being in an abusive relationship later in my twenties before I was a mother, this had more impact on my emotional personality. I could not express my love for anyone and it wasn't until my baby was put in my life that I learned how to do so.

That night at church, like a tsunami, the memories of the molestation flooded my emotions. It overshadowed the physical and emotional battery I experienced in a marriage that was formed out of my downward spiral of depression. After being delivered from the fears and emotional scars of being a battered woman, I couldn't help but wonder why it all came back so strongly and without any warning. Why did his face looking down on me with a smirk in a dark shadowy room, fill my vision?

The memories of being violated suddenly made me sick to the stomach. I took the paper we were given and quickly wrote Harry's name down. I felt a rush of emotions overtake me and I left out of the sanctuary and went to the bathroom. Breaking down in the stall, I cried. Hoping no one would overhear me, I stifled my sobs by holding my hand over my mouth. A flashback of being pinned under him, wanting my Daddy to help me, was causing me anxiety and I began rocking back and forth on the commode. I began speaking to myself, telling myself I was safe and not to be afraid. I was there again after all the years gone by. Not understanding why it was happening, I composed myself and went back into the sanctuary just as the pastor was praying over the notes.

The pastor instructed us to pray a prayer of forgiveness for the name we wrote down then crumble the paper up and toss it into a huge garbage bin. All of this happened on a Friday night. One by one we tossed our notes in the bin. I felt a wave of relief lift up and off of my shoulder. No longer will I carry this thing, this secret and the shame of it all with me. I forgave him and he no longer was in my life controlling my emotions.

Before this night of forgiveness, I had spent the past years employed by the government, traveling and experiencing life working with computers. I had the privilege of being the first African American woman to be positioned on the West Coast in my field of expertise as a Department of Defense Computer Specialist. I loved working with civilians and being connected to the militaries of the United States and overseas. We supplied Desert Storm troops with laptops built to withstand heavy artillery and able to withstand extreme heat and cold. Each of these laptops weighed nearly eleven pounds. I prayed every time we shipped them overseas that we would end the war and bring our troops home. We were told they were also used as a shield against flying shrapnel. I prayed that as they carried these heavy laptops that it would become their full armor shield.

Two days after we had our forgiveness ritual, I went to church on Sunday. The church owned a restaurant where my fellow praise team, choir members and I, would frequent in between services. That morning after the seven thirty service we did our usual thing. When entering the restaurant we noticed a group of people enjoying their meal. Then I saw him sitting in the middle of the group. My heart started beating fast as I tried to avoid him. He noticed me and called me by my childhood name as if to let me know "It's me, I'm back!" I started shaking when he asked me if I went to the church that owned the restaurant and I answered, yes. I, in return, asked if he went to the church and he said no, but his daughter did.

I then remembered seeing a girl with his last name as she was given an award from the youth ministry group, who looked just like him. So it was his daughter. I immediately wondered if he molested his own daughter but I realized that he was a teenager when he molested me. I was only three or four years old, unable to stop him and was helpless to his advances.

I do not remember if I bought any food from the restaurant that day, only that I wanted to leave the place as quickly as I could. Hurrying, I left out the door letting out the breath that I had been holding since I heard my childhood nickname called out and suddenly stopped breathing normally. My breaths then became fast and erratic.

At first I didn't know why all the bad memories of what Harry did came flooding back when asked to forgive the one that hurt you.

None of the physical marital abuse dealt by the hand of my ex came flooding back, probably because I had forgiven him even before asked to do so. Harry showed up within days after the singles service. One of the many memories I have of people, not seen or heard from in years, suddenly appearing before me within days of me thinking of them. There they would be, either standing or sitting right in front of me.

But this specific encounter, God wanted me to overcome because it had altered my personality. Being very defensive but misunderstood, Mom started telling people that I was mean. I didn't know who I was or where I fitted in. At times in my personal life, I felt like that little girl helpless and unsure of herself. I was a fighter, yet easily gave up when engaged by another in my personal life but as a business woman I excelled in everything that I did. Being a quick learner, there was nothing that I put my mind or hand to do that I did not conquer, nothing. There was nothing that I couldn't figure out how to repair or build even without instructions.

Looking back in my past, it was not always easy to walk away from persons that pushed and pressured themselves into my life. When in second grade, I had developed breasts earlier than most second graders. Well let's say all the second, third and some fourth graders. My sister who was in fourth grade had not developed. The circumstance arrived when my mother had to run to K-Mart and pick out a bra for me all because my older brother would no longer let me take my shirt off and get wet like we did every summer. This was the day which forever changed me. When I was child, we all, girls and boys took off our shirts to get wet.

My brother got the hose ready for all the neighborhood kids who gathered anxiously, waiting for that first spray of water from the water hose in our backyard so they could get wet. So, off came all the shirts when my brother hollered my name and told me to keep my shirt on. I tried to disrobe and he came over, pulled my shirt down abruptly while I screamed that I wanted to get wet too. He then told me I could not take my shirt off and I ran in the house to tell Mom. Mom then grabbed her keys and said we were going to K-mart to buy me a bra. As we went to make the purchase, my mom explained to me why I could no longer go shirt-less. None of the older girls had developed and I was the first to get a bra in the neighborhood. I had mixed emotions about being so young and now finding myself the interest of every boy on the street.

At eight years old, I liked bragging about my new bra to the girls. My sister got a bra because she did not want to be left out but at ten she had not yet developed. Mommy told Daddy and he in turn threatened the boys in the neighborhood to leave me alone after he caught one of the boys putting his hand down my shirt. Later in my adult life at about 23, I was told by my neighbor's brother that my oldest brother watched out for me and threatened the other boys with a beat down. He, my brother was tall and known to be a good fighter, winning all of his childhood brawls. It was then I realized why, as a teenager, I couldn't get a date. They were afraid of my brother. I was One-punch's little sister. He was given that nickname after breaking someone's jaw with one punch.

There were seven of us girls who hung out together on our immediate street and fifteen boys who ranged from age nine to sixteen. Until my daddy and brother's threat, I was being harassed by the older boys daily. There was always a boy trying to kiss me or trying to put his hand down my shirt. So, once again, I found myself being traumatized by children who would inappropriately touch me. Daddy had to gather the boys and give them a warning to leave me alone and told them if he caught anyone of them bothering me he would spank them and then go to their parents. I lived in an area where there were both parents in the home. Everyone was Mr. and Mrs. Somebody and they spanked each other's child if they saw them doing something wrong. I became embarrassed about my development, so early in my life I turned to reading books to escape my surroundings. Becoming an introvert, I did not like to be outside and when possible, took lots of naps after reading a book. Peaceful naps without threat of being inappropriately touched.

My dreams were very vivid and very colorful. In them I would ride in a car with my next door neighbor's brother who was the same age as me and also my first childhood crush. The car was a small silver convertible that would take me and my beau to a fancy ball where we would plan to dance. I always had on the most beautiful ballroom dress just like my Mom's. But I never arrived at the dance, we would drive off and once we got around the corner I would wake up. Always I would go quickly back to sleep and dream of being at my front door which was up a long staircase. While looking out the door down the steps, there was a river with a boat waiting for me. I would walk down the steps to the boat and it would move down the river where the neighborhood was like candy land. The trees and bushes were lollipop and suckers. I would get out and walk through them looking for a way out, but end up walking in circles until I went back to the boat waiting for me.

The trip back home always had strong waves that rocked me until it almost toppled me out of the boat but I would hold onto the sides and soon would see the long staircase to my front door. When I reached the first step it was always with so much difficulty. Not until I reached the top would I then look back at the boat and enter my living room to safety. When I awoke, the bed would be wet. I wet the bed until I was nine, which was when I started my menstrual cycle. Daddy and my brother watched over like a hawk when Mother Nature showed up. But with this event, my sister had begun hers earlier, so I didn't feel alone. Mom had to inform the school and they allowed me to stay home and sent my homework for me to do at home. While in the fast class, it allowed me to continue being ahead in most courses.

Mom would be vigilant about making me go to the bathroom before going to bed and wake me to go the bathroom after being asleep for a while. Once I remembered waking up in her bed and it frightened me. I thought Harry had come in the night, taken me out of my bed then put me in Mom and Daddy's bed. I woke up on Daddy's side where he would have me after separating me from my sister. Crying, I walked to the kitchen and tried to remember how I gotten there, calling out to my Mom asking weakly where she was. Sobbing frantically, I ended up searching until I found her in the kitchen. She then explained how she had awakened me to go to the bathroom and because I was so sleepy, put me in bed with her since it was closer. Being slightly too heavy for her, she had trouble picking me up and Daddy worked graveyard shift leaving his side of their bed open for me to lay down.

At eight years old I saw my first nude female. It was a woman dressed in bunny ears and a bunny tail. Our next door neighbor on the other side of us had a studio apartment over their garage that they would rent out to single black men. One day, we were playing in the garage when the current renter came down the steps and discarded some magazines. My playtime usually was staying inside and reading books. My mom would punish me not by just spanking me but making me go outside. I sat on our back porch which was on the side of our house with two steps in the doorway to endure my punishment. When pressure was put on me by my sister and the other girls in the neighborhood, I would join them in playing house in the garage.

Always being the wife of another girl we would arrange the garage to have a bedroom which consisted of an old mattress. We had a kitchen, using old pot and pans discarded by previous renters and a card table and chairs. This day we waited until he went back upstairs to his apartment and we ran to get magazines for our living room to set out for visitors, just like our parents did. When I opened to the first page there was a naked white woman sitting up, showing her breasts. We looked at each other with surprise in our eyes, sat on the steps leading to the upstairs apartment and kept looking at page after page of naked white women doing all kind of things to their breasts. One picture stood out in particular because she had a straw in her mouth and the other end was in her bra. We had been introduced to the popular naked white women magazine of the time.

The women wore white bunny ears and bunny tails with very little clothes on. Our curiosity had us exploring each other's chest areas. I had breasts but not as developed as the white women in the magazine. We were wondering why there was a straw in her mouth. We never took our clothes off to look down between our legs. We knew, we just knew that it was wrong to do that. What was she sipping through the straw that was connected to her bra? I recall being aroused with the same feeling I had when Harry would touch me and tickle me between my legs. We were exposed to nudity through the magazine.

At times after discovering a secret place, I would close the bathroom door and lock it so no one could come in and catch me looking at adult magazines. When looking under the bathroom sink one day for toilet paper, there I found more naked women magazines. I didn't know who they belonged to but later found out they were Daddy's. I carefully put them back just like I had found them. Never did I tell my sister or the other girls that they were there and only would look at them when both Mom and Dad were gone from the house.

New neighbors moved across the street from us and became friends with our parents right away because their father also worked with my Dad. Daddy was the one who told them about the house for rent across the street from us. Daddy was transferred from Davis Relay Station to Sacramento Army Depot as the first black supervisor in the Telecommunications and Data Processing Division. The oldest girl was nine, the same age as my sister, their son was five like my younger brother and the baby girl was three. From Norfolk, Virginia they came into our neighborhood and fit right in with the social life that my parents had. Now since there were older girls to watch us, the sitter changed from Harry to the two older daughters of my parent's friends. They took turns watching over us as our parents socialized on the weekends. The molestation stopped when he couldn't be alone with me any longer. I was about seven by this time.

My oldest brother played with boys that were much older than he was so my sister, younger brother and I didn't spend much time with him. I have very few memories of what my older brother's childhood was like. What we three siblings experienced next was a direct result of our encounters with a three year old girl. There was a consensus between those of us in our neighborhood that this three year old, was a very nasty little girl. Since she was the youngest, we would often pick her up to sit on our laps. She then would proceed to put her hand down the girls' pants and try to fondle them between their legs. When it happened to me, I was completely paralyzed by the act and couldn't move. We tried to tell her older sister, but to no avail. She wouldn't even entertain the thought.

It made me wonder who touched her in that matter. Who taught her to touch other little girls like that? Sleep wouldn't come to me after that incident. This little girl had every one of us running from her and she would chase us just to stick her hand down our pants. Where would she have gotten this behavior? Did it come from her father? Her brother was only five and still being bathed by his mother. It was probably the reason the boy had a terrible stutter. Yeah, I think it was her mother who washed her down there. I didn't understand it then but I felt something was not right with the mom, as a matter of fact I knew it. She always wanted to give the three year old baths to the point that my mother mentioned something to the next door neighbor about it. I overheard them say she probably made her bathe often because the dad wanted her to be spotless when he came home. She was his first child. I didn't like their mother even though I never really understood why.

Their father saw that my five year old brother was cooking fried eggs for us one morning, something my mother taught us all to do at an early age along with the chore of washing dishes. Their father scratched his head in disbelief and said that his wife was babying their five year old by still bathing him. The nine year old and five year old were not his biological children yet the three year old was and he doted on her. I once saw the mother making a strange face and frowning when he called out her name, showing obvious opposition to his show of favoritism. Curiosity had us asking why she looked different and the oldest sister told us that she was his first child and looked more like him, he was light skinned and she was too. She and her brother looked alike, dark complexion with round faces, like their mom. After the two of them, she had remarried then gave birth to their sister. They didn't stay in our neighborhood very long because the father was transferred overseas and just as quickly as they came, they were gone. I will never forget the girl who had all the other girls running from her, running from the hand of a little three year old trying to go down their pants.

The summer had come to an end and school was soon to start. School was a safe haven for me because I didn't have to stay home with my mom. I found out when I was older that my mom suffered from post-partum depression from the birth of my oldest brother and consequently with all four of us. She was ill from having four babies. I was the child who apparently broke her will as my Dad took her while she was sleep and she ended up pregnant. Mom refused to lay with Dad because she didn't want any more of his children, is how she explained it when I was about seven or eight. She always and only disclosed this information when she was drunk at my parents many social gatherings at our house.

Mom always told me that she didn't want me. She said she only wanted two kids but Daddy wanted four. Daddy broke her will when I was conceived. At times when the story was told, I would see the same look that I saw on the face of the mother of that three year old little girl. She once told her friend that was visiting that I was the only one that looked like Daddy and she could not stand looking at me. It was always bad for me when he did something wrong. At a young age, I remember being told that I was not wanted by my mother and looking so much like him made her not want me or respect me even more. That was why I would get spankings which were actually closer to beatings.

Mom would use an extension cord for things that I can't even remember doing. She always hit me with such force it would leave bloody welts on my arms and legs. Before there were antiseptics, we would use iodine or peroxide for cleaning and treating cuts and scrapes. I felt as if the iodine bottle was only bought for me, since I used it the most. It was always ongoing, non-stop spankings while my brother and sister were away at school. I don't remember my sister or older brother getting spankings because they were away in their classes, their safe havens. I couldn't wait until I could go to school. School meant peace of mind, an escape into other places and worlds, away from my mom and her depression.

I once asked my sister when we were in our twenties if Mom ever called her out of her name. She angrily said no and I need to stop lying to her about Mom calling me names. When I told her that she did it in front of a childhood friend, she didn't believe me. After our friend actually confirmed the verbal abuse by our mother, it was even harder to hear my sister say that I probably deserved it. Many times I tried to tell her what Harry did to me, but I felt she wouldn't believe me then either, so I kept it to myself. Never have I said anything to anyone until now that Harry, the person who hurt me, was laid to rest.

In this life's journey I came to know God as my savior. I learned the hard task of forgiveness. Learning that forgiveness is not for the abuser, the perpetrator but for the abused to go forward and prosper in all that life has in store for them. God's grace is sufficient to see them to fruition of all the good he has in store. "And He said unto me, my grace is sufficient for thee: for my strength is made perfect in weakness. Most gladly therefore will I rather glory in my infirmities, that the power of Christ may rest upon me." 2 Corinthians 12:9. Blessings cannot be blocked if we learn how to forgive.

I made up my mind at an early age to never say I hated anyone. Always looking into the hearts of the abuser, but it was not easy. I read that many abusers physically murdered their victims and after I learned that God forgives murderers, I thought I should too, because I was living. What I did not know is that my dreams of success which once came so easily to me were murdered by the abuse. Being that it was so early in my childhood when it took place, I let it kill a lot of my dreams.

I was way ahead of my time. A lot of successful trends in the fashion world came to me when in elementary school. I was labeled the "weird acting little girl" when in fourth grade I would polish my nails to match the colors of my clothing, sometimes polishing them in different directions and multiple colors. The kids would gather around me, asking to see my nails, amazed at the different things I did to them every day.

I created a chart, putting on samples of all the colors to show what I had and then numbered them. That made it easy for me to apply matching colors to my nails. My teachers would tell me to take the polish off when I got home after leaving school and do not come back with them colored. Yet I did it again and again because I loved the attention and the fact that the kids who were beginning to grow taller than me would treat me with kindness. Even the bullies protected me. They made me feel special and I didn't fear being the center of attention. Now I know that God was revealing to me the creativity that was placed in me at my birth. Today, in the 20th century all of the nails salons are doing what I started in elementary school. He showed me that I was ahead of my time but I still didn't live my dreams because of fear. The abused crippled me from stepping into the future God had shown me. I lost focus of that creative part that often leads to the success of so many in the fashion industry. My daddy always said I was going to be a wealthy woman. I know he would have been right if only I had moved into the knowledge my dreams had created for me. Fear is a stronghold that appears to be a truth when in fact it is FEAR, False Evidence Appearing Real.

Before the attention I received in fourth grade over the nails and being called "weird acting", I captured the attention of a different girl when I was just in second grade, unwarranted attention. A girl who started touching, poking and grinding me against the stall walls in the girls bathroom at school. Being molested in second grade by a fourth grade girl who was also a preacher's daughter was devastating. My now safe haven away from my mom was presenting challenges when the fourth grader was fascinated by my developing breasts. In second grade, I was the only girl in school besides my sister, who wore a bra and we bragged to the other neighborhood girls about wearing them. At school my bragging turned to hiding in the girl's bathroom at recess because of this girl. Every time I came through the doors to enter the playground, I would have to duck around corners to avoid her as she was always waiting for me, which started making me ill. My stomach would tighten and I would have headaches from the stress of this new situation. I now know the entire time I was actually having panic attacks.

I didn't tell my sister that her fourth grade classmate would take me to the girls' bathroom and pressure me into letting her feel my breasts. Always avoiding the other girls who were present by dragging me into the last stall in this large bathroom and telling me if I let her touch me she would let me bring my Barbie dolls to her house. She told my sister and me that we could play with her Barbie doll house, so I allowed her to touch my breasts even though I remember how painful they were as they were still developing. While she groped and fondled my aching breasts, I thought of the day we could play with her doll house. After what seemed like months of her cornering me in the girl's bathroom, I asked her when was she going let me and my sister come over.

One day after school as we walked home she said she had asked her Dad if she could play with us on the weekend. He allowed her to come to our house and play. Never touching me while we were at home, she would wait until we were at school. It got to the point where I would play sick and go to the nurse's office during recess but that lasted only for a minute. I couldn't hide out there because they would talk to my parents about being ill so often. We always walked home from school which was five miles. All the kids from the neighborhood walked. Now, not only having to dodge the boys at home but also this girl at school, I was losing a lot of sleep. Feeling that it was wrong for her to be touching me and not knowing how to stop it without losing the chance to play with a real Barbie doll house.

It came to an end the day we walked home and before turning on our block, two blocks before hers; I pulled out my Barbie and said we could come over her house and play. I had already asked my mom and dad if we could go to her house after school. She said it was okay but when we got to her house she ran in and said for us to wait, she first had to ask her dad. When she returned then she told us we could not play today. That was the last time we saw her, because she moved away and was gone over the weekend. I was hurt because she didn't let us play with the doll house but I was happy now that I could play at recess without fear. I no longer had to worry about being grabbed, led into the girls' bathroom and then touched by this girl. I felt safe again.

My school was the safe place for me, at least before the aggravation from this fourth grader, where as home was not. I was afraid to be home alone at night with my mother. Later in my twenties I found out that my mom suffered with a temporary mental illness due to depression, during and after her pregnancies. Knowing this I was able to forgive and love my mom even though I always felt she never loved me.

The 20/20 episode started out with women saying they wanted to hurt their children. Each one recounted how they were feeling. One wanted to push her child down a flight of stairs. Another pushed the hand of her child into the garbage disposal and yet another wanted to drown her child. Mom sat down at the kitchen table where I had the small television turned on, with my bible open, I was reading for comfort. I waited for her to realize that these women were speaking things that she felt but did not understand why she felt that way. With tears in my mom's eyes, she apologized for the horrible feelings she had towards me. She said I was a beautiful baby but she wanted to hurt me. My brother, she had wanted because after multiple miscarriages she prayed for a son. With her second successful pregnancy, she wanted a girl and she got her girl. She was done with her family.

Two successful pregnancies yet she would cry when Daddy left for work and would not stop until he almost returned home. This started from her first delivery with my oldest brother and after each of her deliveries. She didn't know to tell anyone and thought it was just the baby blues as it was called and that it would soon pass. She didn't understand why she cried when holding her beautiful son and later her daughter. She didn't want any more babies and she was slowly recovering from the pregnancies. So when she woke up one morning obvious sign of intimacy she knew had occurred, she cried.

She knew she was pregnant with her third. She told her friends how she had known our father had taking advantage of her while sleeping. I realized when I was older that Mom cut intimacy with him and he strayed but always loved her and wanted to be with his wife.

Mom apologized for spanking me harder than the others and at times out of control which led to bloody welts. She apologized, asked me to forgive her and I said I did and asked her to stop crying. Despite all the times I had wished I never been born because the abuse was unbearable. I remembered mom accidently suffocated me with a pillow because I was screaming so loudly and fighting her back. She revived me in a bathtub of cold water. I remember sitting in the bathtub, soaking wet with my clothes on and Mom muttering to herself. Later I sat at the kitchen table in my bathrobe eating ice cream and cookies trying to remember why I was even in the bathtub in the first place. I couldn't, until years had passed, recall why at the time my mom was being so kind to me. My brother and sister were away in school which is where I longed to be, in school where all the big kids went to get away from their moms and dads.

I barely shed tears anymore by the time I was five due to multiple spankings. My younger brother would cry to stop my mom from spanking me. He told me when he was about eight years old that he cried for me because I wouldn't. He asked me why I wouldn't cry because crying was how he got her to stop spanking him. I would stand watching her hit me as she got madder and became more violent by switching the belt to an extension cord. Why didn't I cry? This would have stopped the abuse. Being in the midst of it, is seemed impossible to see a way out of it so I became angry, developing a temper which would at times be uncontrollable.

My older brother and sister didn't understand my temper but my younger brother did. What he did not understand is why I had stopped the tears from falling. Not until when we were older did I tell him the things that our mom had done to me. He said he remembered some things but had no idea why Mom acted as if she did not like me. One thing he did understand is that he was able to get away with a lot, which led him to doing things that caused Mom a lot of grief. He almost made me feel that he did things to give her stress in order to get back at her for what she had done to me. He saw more than my two older siblings saw yet didn't believe when I tried to tell them. My older brother wasn't aware of any of our mom's issues; at least he denied ever knowing, so I couldn't tell him anything. He always blamed me for the tension between my mother and I.

After many arguments that I couldn't count if I tried, one of the most memorable memories I have is when, as adults, I planned an all girls weekend trip to Los Angeles. Wanting to break in my new car, a Toyota Camry, I told my sister that we could take a trip to LA and my mother was welcome to come. I felt with my sister being there, we could have a pleasant trip as Mom didn't attack me verbally when my sister was around.

Mom constantly talked about how uppity I was with my light skin that would have gotten me in the blue bloods society in Louisiana where she was born. My sister who was dark skinned, always walked with her head down and Mom took it as low self-esteem. But I always walked with my head up and smiled a lot. The blue bloods were an old Creole social club that would allow you to join if you were lighter than a brown paper bag and you could see the blue veins in your wrists. Apparently it was an organization in which I was accepted to be a member, without ever applying to the club. My mom constantly mentioned that I thought I was better than my sister. My sister loved me and I loved her so much but our mom told my sister that I thought she was beneath me. When we were away from Mom, I told her that I did not ever feel or think that way.

Recalling an incident, as adults, while getting tires for my sister's car she brought up the fact that she felt light skinned girls always acted as if they were better than then dark skinned girls and were stuck up. I said I was light skinned and didn't think I was better and that I was not stuck up. She blinked, stared at me as if she was seeing me for the first time and agreed that no, I was not like the others and that she knew I loved her. We both began to cry and with tears in our eyes we hugged each other. In the midst of our conversation, a dark skinned girl walked up to the counter where we waited for tires to be mounted on my sister's car. The girl looked at me and rolled her eyes and then looked at my sister and greeted her. My sister looked over at me and smiled. She understood I was being treated unkindly just because I was light skinned.

For years I felt verbally abused by my mother because I was different from and didn't act like my sister. I found out that holding our heads up high was part of my Dad's family makeup. At a family reunion on my father's side I noticed that most of my relatives sat proudly. I no longer was ashamed to hold my head high as it was my inherited family trait but having that trait seemed to give my mom a reason to disrespect me in public. Once she said loudly in a crowd of strangers waiting in line at the grocery store, how stuck up I was as I walked to get in line. It didn't bother me anymore and I ignored her which made her angry but by this time I was grown and not easily intimidated. This time there was no reaction that satisfied her so we drove home in silence.

The same happened on our trip to Los Angeles my mom consistently verbally attacked me for no reason. As my sister drove, I couldn't enjoy the music that played on the radio without my mother bursting out over singing me. Mom had a beautiful operatic voice and that day was using every decibel she had, to drown out mine. Even though I was known to sing in the neighborhood every morning, Mom never once let me know that she appreciated my singing. My sister had a melodic alto voice and we would sing together. Mom heard her singing one day and told our neighbor that she knew my sister could sing but that I always tried to overshadow her because I was jealous. So much verbal abuse went on I can't remember half of it. All I do remember is trying to sleep so I would not be bothered with listening to her. My sister drove the entire way to LA. Once we got to our cousin's house the excitement that I felt was quickly quenched when after eating dinner, Mom began to dig into me again.

Our cousin lived in Bowling Hills of Los Angeles where famous music legends had their homes up the street and around the corner from her. I couldn't wait until we started our day of shopping at the garment district where street merchants and local business owners gave you the best deals after you bartered with them but that day never came. The next morning we all woke up and sat down to have breakfast. Cousin Joyce had homemade biscuits, eggs and sausage and feeling all of the love in the room, my mother decided to try and make this a happy moment. She told cousin that I was good at telling if a transaction or situation would go in one's favor. I told her all I could feel about the situation she was in and that all would be well. My cousin was comforted by I had said but then Mom suddenly began bringing up my past. She said yes I was accurate in a lot of what I felt but that I had a bad temper. A temper that was usually brought on by Mom causing me to become defensive, irritated and unable to relax and enjoy the moment, exactly like this. Now she was making me uncomfortable and put me again, in that unhappy place, the very place I thought I was escaping by planning a trip for us.

After breakfast we headed out the door to get in the car and my sister sat in the driver's seat warming it up. She did something that I asked her never to do which was pressing on the gas pedal to speed up the process. I called out for her to take her foot off of the gas and my mom told me to leave her alone. Angrily she said I didn't need to teach my sister how to drive because she already drove better than I did. Now irritated, I told Mom that she needed to learn not to gas pedal a car with fuel injection as it would cause a problem with the injection valve. Why did I say something that she did not understand? Now I had opened a mess of revengeful statements about how I again thought I was better than my sister. It was becoming too much a challenge trying to be happy with Mom on the trip and I just wanted to go home, back to my house and the peace of being left alone.

I quickly climbed into the backseat of my car while my mom sat in the front seat with my sister as the designated driver. We started down the hill to Crenshaw Blvd to and the local drugstore, I needed aspirin because of a terrible headache that wasn't getting any better. My sister and I went inside the drugstore while mom staying in the car and waited for our return. Once inside, we located what I needed and went to the cashier. We were pleasantly surprised to see so many blacks working in the store which was unlike our hometown of Sacramento.

At the checkout stand the woman bagging groceries for the person in front of us started to noticeably stare at me, instead of the person she was helping. Looking at my sister, I raised my eyebrows to let her know something was up with the lady. My sister stared at the lady with her shoulders back and head up, trying to get her to break the unnerving stare. All of the sudden the woman stuck out her tongue and clasped the side of her mouth, the tell tale sign of a lesbian wanting to have sex with you. I directed my stare to the ground, my sister paid for my aspirin and we walked quickly to the car. Once back at the car I asked her if she had seen the same thing I did.

My sister then told Mom what we just witnessed and she could not believe it. We both explained to her what signals lesbians and homosexuals used to get the attention of others that they wanted to have sex with. We learned the signals from one of our childhood friends who was a lesbian. Her parents were both bi-sexual and gave room and board to local transgender males and cross dressers.

This friend tried to convince me at the age of sixteen to try being with a woman. She stated that I would make a good lesbian because I had facial hair and that, to her, was very attractive. I disagreed. I liked and preferred the male anatomy and wanted to explore it more, I was already familiar with a female and what went on in our vagina, I was one. It didn't turn me on instead it made me cringe to think about it. It would require a man to wash out his mouth after an act with a woman's genitals. If bleach was safe to use I would have him use it even if the act was performed on me.

As we drove to the garment district to go shopping, Mom did not appreciate the peaceful silence we were enjoying. She started saying just without provocation the phrase "End of conversation!" Repeating the phrase over again until my sister started laughing. I didn't laugh because I didn't know why she was making the statement so I asked my sister what Mom meant by it. Laughing, Mom said that it's what I said whenever I wanted to end an argument. Then she made more references to me being mean and wanting to control every argument by stating when we should stop. Over and over mom kept digging at me.

Well it was end of conversation and the trip. I told my sister to turn around and go back to our cousin's house so we can pack and go home. This was enough of our girls' weekend trip. When she didn't turn right away, I started screaming that I was done.

Once at the house our cousin was surprised to see us back so early and she immediately noticed that I was agitated. I quickly packed my bags and threw them in the trunk. Turning to her, I apologized, said that the trip was over and we were leaving right now for home. They packed and got in the car, my sister once again got in the driver's seat. I asked her to move over and let me drive and then we were on our way. A normally eight hour drive ended up taking five and I was in my sanctuary, never to attempt a girls weekend out again.

Finally alone, I cried with a vengeance and starting throwing up. Never would I say I hated my mother because I did not, but no one could convince me that she loved me or that I loved her. Especially since love was very unfamiliar to me. The only family that I knew loved me was my sister who was tired of being the cushion between me and Mom tearing into each other, my father and my maternal grandmother, mom's mother who loved me and showed it. They were the only reasons I learned to love someone and became confident with myself. Loving me was hard to do without an example to follow. But then I allowed God to enter my heart and amazing women helped me to see how He saw me and through studying His word, began to believe it. Believing allowed me to act on it and receive love.

Mother's day was a depressing time when it came to choosing a special card. There was no card expressing how I felt about her. The cards were always too appreciative of her and no way captured my true feelings. So I would buy a nice blouse or some jewelry, leaving the card to my sister who would have me sign my name. Mom always thought I was trying to outdo my sister with a card and a gift, stating it verbally. My sister knew what I was feeling because I told once when we went card shopping, muttering to myself about how wrong the cards were. They didn't tell how I felt but it was good that they didn't, there would have been an argument like no other one we ever had. It was hard to make Mother's Day a happy day with my mother, at the same time it came so easy for me and my grandmother. She always looked forward to the card which made her smile and she always complimented me on my handwriting. She only had a third grade education but at 75 years old, received home schooling, graduating from 5th grade. I was so proud of Meme.

Meme, born in Louisiana, spoke Creole and broken English with a heavy accent. All of our friends didn't understand her and I always interpreted for her. Being her granddaughter I thought she spoke perfect English and laughed when others couldn't understand her. People laughed because when she became frustrated would say "shhoott" which came out sounding like "shit" or so I thought for most of my life. Later I found out that shit was a commonly used explicative expression when she was a child in Louisiana amongst the Creole and Cajun people. It was as common as the word "what?" It made me laugh when I remember all the times I said "No, she is saying shoot" but in reality was saying "shit".

When Mother's Day was over, I could relax after being with my maternal grandmother and then sleep at night peaceably because of my grandmother's love. Always I could be myself and she loved who I was as myself.

Now after remembering traumatic experiences of my past from early childhood to adulthood, I have learned to love who I am and stand strong from all the experiences I have lived through. God has shown me how to love myself and how to forgive others who have hurt me. The experiences, good and bad, have helped me to be who I am today. Knowing who I am was not an easy task. Hiding behind fake smiles at home with my friends and on the job helped me fool a lot of people. When as an adult, I got into relationships never expecting anyone man or woman to be faithful in any way, trusting no one. Turning to the church, I found the only one I could trust was God. I tried Him and proved Him to be true.

In my late teens years I had become suicidal. Feeling unloved by my mother, I could no longer take her constant pursuit to alienate me from knowing what love was. I became tired and weary of trying but when I began reading the King James Version of the Bible; I began to understand that the bible was color blind. It placed mankind as a whole and told us to repent and turn from our wicked ways. God also said that He was love and He loved us unconditionally. "He that loveth not knoweth not God; for God is love." 1 John 4:8. I learned of his infinite love towards us as each page I turned showed examples of his love.

He showed me unconditional love that I never knew. Jeremiah 1:5 states "Before I formed you in the womb I knew [and] approved of you [as My chosen instrument], and before you were born I separated and set you apart, consecrating you; [and] I appointed you as a prophet to the nations." was the first word of God that set my path to victory. How can I attain this for my life, was the next question I asked. God's responses came as I asked, I dropped open the bible and looked down at the answer. It was amazing to me the journey that I was now pursuing. His answer to this was found in 2 Chronicles 7:14. "If my people, which are called by my name, shall humble themselves, and pray, and seek my face, and turn from their wicked ways; then will I hear from heaven, and will forgive their sin, and will heal their land." This word was so refreshing, just like drinking a tall cold glass of water, so satisfying and easy to follow. I was not a person who sought to do bad things or was revengeful. The love I stored up for years was finally being tapped into and released by learning the Bible but the best thing was that I believed in God's word. I tried it and it worked.

I learned that I had entered into a world of living without fear, because He loved me and took care of my needs and gave me some of my wants. He told me in my dreams which were very vivid to fear not and stop looking behind in my past. Stop playing the hurts over and over in my head. God did not want me to be discouraged in thinking that I will never be loved but there was one thing I could not understand and that was how to love. How to trust anyone and then after dropping the Bible, it opened to this verse in 2 Timothy 1:7 "For God hath not given us the spirit of fear; but of power, and of love, and of a sound mind." Then the scripture in Romans 12:1-2,

"I beseech you therefore, brethren, by the mercies of God, that ye present your bodies a living sacrifice, holy, acceptable unto God, which is your reasonable service. And be not conformed to this world: but be ye transformed by the renewing of your mind, that ye may prove what is that good, and acceptable, and perfect, will of God."

Romans 12:1-2 became my foundational scripture, meaning that I studied it every day. Being now of sound mind, no longer suicidal and feeling unloved, I stopped dwelling or allowing the hurts of my childhood to control me and began learning about being the woman that God wanted me to be. Although there was times that I was unsure if I was doing the right thing, I knew God's love covered me to know repentance sets things back on the right path and strength and His forgiveness allowed it to be. Victory is mine! Love is mine, peace is mine, joy is mine as I believe to this day because I am somebody and nothing can separate me from the love of Christ.

For His love has taught me that we learn from our past but do not dwell in it. Our past made us strong, who we are today and though it was hurtful, we made it through all the bad things. We are made whole through the washing of God's word, which means we need to 2 Timothy 2:15 "Study to shew thyself approved unto God, a workman that needeth not to be ashamed, rightly dividing the word of truth." Victory came for me when I chose to let go of my past and believe what the word of God says. "And ye shall know the truth, and the truth shall make you free." John 8:32. The hurt in my past has not defined me as a person but has come to make me strong and to help others overcome their situations. Knowing this is why I am writing about the things that happened to me. No longer bound by my past, I was able to forgive and love those that hurt me.

I truly love my mother and know she is in heaven because she loved me back while I took care of her until her last breath of life. My sister left for heaven in 2003, an untimely death dealt by the hands of someone she trusted, someone that my mother and I have forgiven together so that God could help us move on together. I no longer felt alone. I no longer feared my mother's provoking ways. I truly forgave those who molested me and pray that they have made it and will go to Heaven like I know Harry and Momma have. Blessed be to God of Glory, to whom all blessings flow from heaven to us on earth. Believe and receive because they are yours to take if we are obedient to His word. God has given to us freely all that we need to live successful, victorious lives, so take control of what has been given. Joy, Love and Peace are ours, if we believe. God bless!

Anna Marie

Your Own Tears
By
Anna Marie

I've seen women sinking in sadness
In danger of drowning in tears
I know that women have died here
In the depths of depression
The pit of loneliness, too many accustomed to darkness

I've heard them cry "freedom"
Imprisoned in marriages to men who've martyred themselves
Self made masters of misery, dealers of deception and pain
I've seen queens changed by demeaning words and curses until
Their heads hang in shame and they doubt their own worth
Used, abused, dissed then dismissed
Too many young girls these days answer to bitch like its okay

These figurines of real men sculpt insults from falsifications
On makeshift pedestals, stroking their egos by putting us down
But we're tired of going round in circles
We've all had high hopes only to be followed by heartaches
But we still sat waiting, anticipating fake apologies
Saying I'm sorry doesn't fix a thing

He has stripped you down to feelings
Dangles dreams of a ring on a string without intention
Because he'd rather keep the collar around your neck
But only you know when to let go, when enough is enough
I know it's tough to walk away
But is worse to let things stay, the way they are

See, the moon makes the tides change
Years make the times change
But the only thing that can change someone's ways is their will
Yet still you try cause it's easier to fall in love than out of
And you're afraid of learning to trust all over again
Or whatever it is
It can't be worse than drowning...
In your own tears

I give the highest praise to our Lord and Savior, by His grace we been given the strength to endure and the blessing of survival. My deepest appreciation goes out to each and every woman whom has bared her soul and told her story through tears, one tablespoon at a time. This book would not have come to be without your courage and willingness to become the voice for all women whom haven't yet found theirs. Thank you.

(Printed by permission of)

Caroline Swanson
Linda LeMaire
Dana D'Amico
Kelly Freeman
Denice Jones
Brittany Hill

Anna Marie

CPSIA information can be obtained
at www.ICGtesting.com
Printed in the USA
FSOW02n1830270715
9121FS

9 780996 114622